Guitar Technique

INTERMEDIATE TO ADVANCED

HECTOR QUINE

OXFORD UNIVERSITY PRESS
1990

Oxford University Press, Walton Street, Oxford OX2 6DP

Oxford New York Toronto
Delhi Bombay Calcutta Madras Karachi
Petaling Jaya Singapore Hong Kong Tokyo
Nairobi Dar es Salaam Cape Town
Melbourne Auckland

and associated companies in
Berlin Ibadan

Oxford is a trade mark of Oxford University Press

Published in the United States
by Oxford University Press, New York

© Hector Quine 1990

British Library Cataloguing in Publication Data

Quine, Hector, 1926—
Guitar technique: intermediate to advanced.
1. Guitar playing techniques
I. Title
787.6' 1' 0714
ISBN 0–19–816211–1
ISBN 0–19–322323–6 (Pbk)

Library of Congress Cataloging in Publication Data

Quine, Hector.
Guitar technique: intermediate to advanced/Hector Quine.
1. Guitar— Instruction and study. I. Title.
MT580.Q56   1990   787.87'193 — dc20   89–23232
ISBN 0–19–816211–1
ISBN 0–19–322323–6 (Pbk)

Typeset by Hope Services (Abingdon) Ltd.
Printed in Great Britain by Biddles Ltd.,
Guildford and King's Lynn

Contents

INTRODUCTION

A BOOK with the title 'Guitar Technique' needs to begin with a definition of the word 'technique', since the term is frequently misunderstood or misapplied. Guitarists are often heard to refer to a player as having a 'good technique' when all that he has in reality is a measure of finger dexterity or the stamina to play pieces of acknowledged difficulty—usually at a rather faster speed than musical coherence suggests. This is the kind of 'virtuoso' of whom Beethoven said: 'All reason and feeling are generally lost in the nimbleness of his fingers.' A century earlier, Couperin expressed much the same view but in different terms: 'I declare in all good faith, that I am more pleased with what moves me than with what astonishes me.'

Technique, in the true sense of the word, is neither the ability to struggle through a lengthy or difficult work—like scaling a high mountain—nor does it imply an athletic contest intended to demonstrate the facility to play a particular passage faster than, or at least as fast as, a well-known performer, regardless of musical sense. Technique is essentially control: control of tone, volume, rhythm and tempo, legato and staccato, dynamics and registration, phrasing and articulation; always consciously directed by musical intelligence. Such control of every detail of performance is just as necessary whether the piece of music be long or short, easy or difficult, fast or slow, and its mastery is an indication that the player has reached a point in his development when he has acquired the vital technical foundation upon which to build real musicianship.

Technique must never be regarded as an end in itself—or indeed, as an end at all—for it is merely the means to an end. Practising begins in the mind; thoughtless mechanical routine can only retard progress and instil faults which are very difficult, if not impossible, to eliminate later.

It is my intention in this book to describe the technical

principles upon which the best current practice in guitar-playing is founded, and to explain the reasoning behind these principles. The book is not a 'method' (a term implying dogma without explanation); I would prefer to think of it as an essentially practical guide, devoid of those 'scientific' theories which guitarists find barely comprehensible and of little relevance. I have tried too, to avoid the airy and fanciful nineteenth-century rhetoric to which some writers on guitar topics seem to be addicted. A passage from a tutor by the renowned piano-teacher Tobias Matthay (1858–1945) illustrates the style: 'all touch, including staccatissimo, must contain this element of resting, or else its correlative (or substitutionary-parallelism)—the resumption of the key-contact (the resumption of the sense of resistance) as a preliminary to each tone production'. More recently, at least two guitar books written in this kind of grandiloquent but opaque prose have appeared on the market.

A clear and simple explanation of anything sometimes meets with the response: 'That is obvious, everyone knows it!' Whether they *did* know it is at least questionable, but in any case they are unlikely to have given the proposition much thought, or to have acted systematically on the consequences. Everything is obvious once it has been pointed out; even Sir Isaac Newton, a scientist of more than average intellect, did not suspect the existence of gravity until an apple fell on his head! It is hard to believe that gravity, being such a commonplace phenomenon, had not been recognized and understood from the dawn of history, yet the obvious only became so after it had been explained. Furthermore, it needed very clear and careful explanation; few people would have made the same deductions as Newton did.

And so it is with guitar technique; most guitarists are convinced that their method alone is correct. The excessive egotism from which many seem to suffer may help to explain why the claim to being 'self-taught' is heard so often. The judge who remarked drily that 'The defendant who conducts his own case has a fool for a client!', could have applied the same logic to self-taught guitarists.

The playing of the most famous guitarist of this century was, in the view of many non-guitarist musicians, eccentric and at variance with musical tradition. To paraphrase Dr Johnson: 'There was a time, not long ago, when musicians regarded guitar-playing as like a dog walking on its hind legs. It is not done well, but you are surprised to find it done at all!'

Times change, and many, if not most, contemporary guitarists recognize the need for the sound basis of musicianship which has been accepted as a standard requirement by other musicians for many decades. My hope is that this book will help to take such progress another step forward. It is not specifically directed at the beginner or elementary player,[1] but the more experienced guitarist should find that the analytical material, which is occasionally controversial, has the positive advantage of stimulating thought, helping him to reappraise his technique and to develop his own performing style within the framework of a clearly defined set of technical principles.

[1] See my *Introduction to the Guitar* (Oxford, 1971).

THE PHYSIOLOGY OF TECHNIQUE

THE Oxford dictionary defines physiology as 'the science of normal functions of living things'. This definition sums up what I believe to be the fundamental principle of all 'mechanical' techniques—whether of playing the guitar, or any other activity which involves trained actions by the human body. The word 'mechanical' may not please everyone, because most people do not like to think of themselves as machines, but the human body is, in reality, a superbly designed and constructed piece of engineering with all the attributes of a machine. (It goes without saying that it also has many other qualities which machines lack.)

In order to make the most efficient use of this 'machine', one must study its most natural functions and plan one's technique accordingly, so moulding and training the strongest and most dependable movements of arms, hands, and fingers as to adapt them to the demands of guitar-playing. Thus, after many hours of systematic, painstaking practising, what has been achieved will *seem* to be a completely natural and relaxed technique.

A great deal has been written and said on the subject of developing a 'natural' technique, and about relaxation in the performance of music, but much of this is misleading. To say that the best use should be made of one's natural physical characteristics is not at all the same as saying that one must always do 'what comes naturally'. Nobody is born with the ability to play the guitar; neither is it possible to learn to play simply by picking up a guitar and letting the fingers do what they will. Using such an approach, even the most naturally gifted beginner would necessarily waste a great deal of time and effort, and make little progress.

Watching and listening to an expert performer, it is easy to misunderstand the nature and function of relaxation; everything appears to be so easy to him that it would seem that the secret of his technique must be that he is completely relaxed. This clearly cannot be so, for if he were to be in a state of absolute relaxation he would not be playing the guitar at all! He would not even be sitting, but lying down motionless! So, many of his muscles must be in a state of tension, and the only conclusion to be drawn from his seemingly nonchalant performance must be that some muscles are relaxed, while others are tensed yet *appear* to be relaxed. How can one appear relaxed while being tense? Three conditions need to be fulfilled:

1 Control of the muscles which have to work independently from those which do not
2 Reserves of strength in excess of that which is needed to perform the task
3 Economy of movement

These are all physiological factors, since it is obviously easier to control muscles efficiently if they are only required to work in ways which are natural to them. It is also easier to isolate surrounding muscles from the action, thereby allowing them to relax; a more powerful muscle, exerting direct effort, is more readily trained. Failure to exercise economy of movement is almost always due to undisciplined or uncoordinated actions which involve several joints and muscles unnecessarily.

A physiological fact which applies to all aspects of technique is that the incorrect use of a more powerful muscle never allows the correct, or weaker, muscle to develop its maximum strength, as essential exercising is thereby avoided. The body's natural reaction when stress is placed on any undeveloped muscle is to call on a stronger one to take the strain. For example, if the grip between index finger and thumb is too weak to hold a barré chord, there is a tendency for the arm to help by pulling, thus making use of the biceps. Therefore, the finger and thumb muscles never do become strong, as they are bypassed instead of being exercised. Only correctly directed exercise can strengthen muscles.

The joints of fingers, wrists, and arms are all able to perform two or more distinct actions, referred to throughout this book as 'primary' and 'secondary' movements. A simple experiment will illustrate the difference: clench the fingers to make a fist;

this I describe as 'moving the fingers along the line of the arm', or their primary movement. Now straighten them again, and, keeping them straight, spread them fanwise to their fullest extent. This is their secondary movement. It is obvious that the first action has far more power and scope of movement than the second, which is both restricted and relatively weak. A technique which relied exclusively on the secondary function would be incapable of being developed to a high level.

The requirements of guitar-playing call for an unbelievable complexity of control and co-ordination, involving some seventy muscles and an equal number of tendons in an infinite number of combinations. The task of the brain in guiding the hands with the utmost precision is almost beyond comprehension, but, fortunately, practising and countless repetition will allow many of the required actions to be regulated entirely by the subconscious mind. It is vital that the design of all movements should be of the simplest and most economical so that the process of transferring them from the conscious to the subconscious part of the brain (practising) can be achieved in the shortest possible time.

To sum up: the simplest movement is the best, and has the greatest potential for continuing progress. This principle governs all aspects of technique, from basic posture to the most advanced levels of finger control of both hands.

POSTURE

A COMFORTABLY balanced sitting posture is of fundamental importance to the development of a sound technique; arms, hands, and fingers can only work efficiently from a stable base, which a sitting position free from unnecessary tension provides.

Faulty posture, a fairly common problem for guitarists, is often due to unequal distribution of bodily weight (see Fig. 1); there is a tendency to lean to one side—usually the left—so that the back is curved instead of being kept straight from the hips to the neck (see Fig. 2). This fault can be caused by too low a chair or too low a footstool; the left knee being allowed to point outwards (or inwards) instead of remaining on the centre line of the body (see Fig. 3).

The principle of the 'three-point' grip of the guitar is, I believe, now so well known as to make it unnecessary for me to deal with it at great length, but a brief restatement of this principle might help to establish the concept of a natural, physiologically sound technique.

The guitar must be supported without help from the hands, which must be free to perform their tasks; any stress caused by gripping the instrument will inhibit their correct actions. For this reason, the guitar is held in a 'clamp' which comprises three points. The most important of these is the left leg, which is positioned with the inside of the calf perpendicular, and on the centre line of the player's body (see Fig. 4). Its role is to provide a (passively) static base against which the guitar is lightly pressed by inward pressure from the right leg. This pressure tends to cause the guitar's lower bout to rise. This tendency is countered by the *weight* of the right forearm resting on the front edge of the guitar. I stress the word 'weight', because a common mistake is to allow the arm to press downwards, involving muscular tension from the shoulder, instead of merely resting its weight on the guitar. When this happens,

Fig. 1

Fig. 2

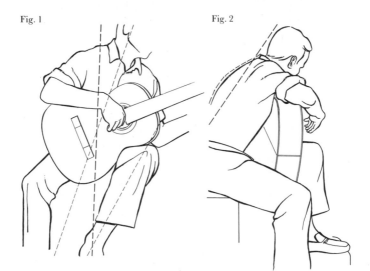

Fig. 3

Fig. 4

the right shoulder will be raised rather than remaining in the same line (parallel to the floor) as the left shoulder. If the guitar is correctly gripped between the right arm's weight, exactly counterbalanced by the slight inward pressure of the right leg—the left leg remaining still—it will be very secure. Apart from the very slight pressure from the right leg, no muscular effort is needed to maintain its position. For several reasons, both technical and physiological, the face of the guitar's soundboard must be held vertically rather than sloping backwards towards the player's body. Leaning the trunk slightly forwards from the hip joints will allow light contact to be made between the chest and the back of the guitar; this supplementary supporting-point will keep the guitar perpendicular and, at the same time, improve the posture by throwing the weight of the player's body forwards. I should emphasize that the back, from the base of the spine to the neck, must maintain its naturally straight posture.

When seen from directly above—a 'bird's-eye' view—the line of the guitar in relation to the player's body should form an acute angle (see Fig. 5). It will become clear (in Chap. 5 on the left hand), that this angle has an important bearing on the efficient use of arm, hand, and fingers. The easiest way of positioning the guitar correctly in this plane is to place the under-side of its 'waist' flat against the inside of the left thigh: because the thigh tapers towards the knee, the instrument will automatically be held at a shallow angle to the chest. I am of course aware that physical characteristics vary considerably from one person to another, but the general principle will always hold good if a slight adjustment is made to allow for this. Care must be taken to see that the (player's) body is not twisted in a leftward direction. When so placed the guitar should need neither pressure nor 'pull' from either the right arm or the left hand to maintain its position.

The angle of elevation of the guitar to the horizontal plane (see Fig. 6) is also dependent to some extent upon the player's physique, though, similarly, the limits are fairly closely defined. The basic need for maximum stability with minimum muscular effort must always be the guiding principle. As a general guide, with the right upper arm fully extended from shoulder to elbow, the arm should be resting at approximately

Fig. 5   Fig. 6

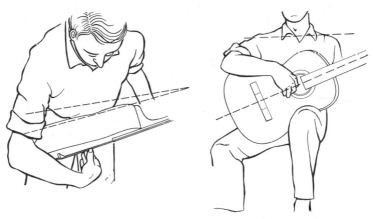

the highest point of the guitar's lower bout. If the chair and footstool are correctly adjusted, the ivory nut at the top end of the fingerboard should be about level with the player's left ear. Too shallow an angle causes (or is caused by) leaning too far to the left instead of sitting with the weight centrally balanced, while too steep an angle causes technical and tonal problems for both hands. The grip of the guitar is also affected, and therefore its stability.

Until it has become a completely subconscious habit, there should be a constant awareness while practising of the need to keep the right leg leaning inwards against the guitar. This helps to instil confidence and certainty to the action of both hands by ensuring that the instrument is securely held. The almost incredible degree of precision needed to play the guitar—particularly in the case of the right-hand fingers, which must be accurate in their stroke to within 1 mm. or less—demands a rock-steady position of the strings, and hence of the guitar itself.

I am a firm believer in the use of a mirror while practising. A few minutes spent in studying posture and grip before beginning to play, and from time to time between scales, exercises etc., is invaluable in helping to identify and eliminate many baffling technical problems. Much else besides posture can be viewed critically and corrected during playing, because the reflected image gives a much better perspective and reveals defective actions in both hands which would not be noticed when looking at them directly. A more subtle, but nonetheless important, advantage of habitual use of the mirror is that the player is compelled to look straight ahead instead of at his left hand—a very common bad habit—and is therefore encouraged to sit up straight! Sitting hunched over the guitar with the nose almost touching the fingerboard is conducive neither to good posture nor to secure, confident playing. This cramped position is more likely when playing from memory than when reading from music. In my experience, guitarists generally place the music-stand far too low and too much in front. A more logical place for the stand is at eye level, so that the player is sitting as straight as a correct posture will allow. Also, placing it to the left rather than centrally will make the occasional glance at the left hand easier without the need for turning the head. This positioning of the music-stand allows a better view of the player by the audience, and vice versa, and encourages a sense of communication and projection by the performer. Many guitarists—particularly amateurs—are inclined to adopt an introverted, 'curled-up' posture which shows only the top of the head to the audience and gives an impression of private self-communing! A stray thought: introverts do not make the best communicators, and music is very much an art of communication!

To sum up: a correct posture and grip of the guitar are the essential foundation for a dependable and co-ordinated technique, and they can only be disregarded by the beginner (or any other player) at his peril. Many guitarists can testify to the anguish of trying to remedy defects in their technique which have been acquired and become fixed by several years of slipshod playing.

Should you be in the unfortunate position of feeling that your technical method is in need of some revision, let me offer a word of encouragement. Do not allow yourself to become depressed during this 'rebuilding' period if you seem to be making little progress—or even going backwards! Remember that when the foundations of a building are being laid, very little shows above the ground, but the essential basis is being established for all later development; take heart also from the old Chinese proverb which says that: 'The longest journey begins with the first step.'

4

RIGHT ARM AND HAND

WE have seen from the remarks concerning posture and grip how the right arm, placed on the edge of the guitar, provides one of the three main points of support for the instrument. It has another, and no less important function: to provide a stable 'base' for the complex and precise movements of hand and fingers, which, as I have said, need to perform to within an accuracy of a millimetre or even less. The effect of a 'floating' right arm on this degree of precision can be imagined, particularly as, applying the principle of leverage, any movement at the elbow is greatly magnified at the fingertip. Instability at the 'pivoting-point' (i.e. the point of contact between arm and guitar edge) causes a feeling of insecurity, which in turn makes for weak and tentative playing, or tensing of the arm in the attempt to maintain a fixed position.

Stability of the right arm depends, to some extent, upon the exact location of the point of contact with the guitar. If the whole arm—fully extended from shoulder to elbow—is allowed to relax completely, so that the arm's 'dead weight' is supported only by the edge of the guitar, a point can be found at which the forearm and upper arm balance each other, with the guitar edge acting as the point of balance. This point is normally just in front of the elbow joint on the forearm, although a player with a very long arm may find that it lies a little further away from the elbow. A simple test will show whether the point has been correctly located: a minimum of effort applied to the hand in a downward direction should cause a rocking motion of the arm, like a finely balanced pair of scales.

A word of warning may be appropriate here. If the guitar itself is slightly unstable due to faulty positioning, there may be an instinctive tendency to correct this either by pressing downwards with the arm instead of simply allowing its weight to rest on the guitar, or, more seriously, by pulling backwards with the elbow, attempting to wedge the guitar against the body. Careful attention to these possible faults will, in a very short time, eliminate them, together with all unnecessary tension in the arm, which should be in a state of rest on the guitar, as it might be if one were to be sitting in a comfortable chair with the elbow resting upon its arm. From this essential starting-point can be developed a playing position for the right hand which is free of needless tension—the key to ultimate technical fluency.

There are many different ways of positioning the right hand in relation to the strings, but to have any real value as technical principles they must satisfy two basic criteria. First, when the hand is in a state of rest (i.e. not actually playing), there should be no muscular tension at all in arm, wrist, or hand. Second, the hand must be positioned so as to allow the production of the optimum tone quality of which player and guitar are capable. It is of course possible, with long practice, to accustom oneself to almost any degree of physical discomfort and tension, but a strained or unnatural position cannot really form a reasonable basis upon which to build a fluent technique; nor will it allow cultivation of the finest tone production and the whole spectrum of tone colour which a properly co-ordinated and balanced right hand makes possible.

A brief consideration of the wrist joint shows that it has (like the fingers, as illustrated in Chap. 2 on physiology) two possible movements: forwards and backwards is the primary function, which has the greatest scope and flexibility. The secondary, or side-to-side, movement is much more limited in both power and latitude, and therefore in usefulness; it is rarely, if ever, used alone in any normal function of the wrist, and appears to exist only in order to permit—when combined with the primary function—a 'rotary' movement of this joint.

A hand position based on a rightward twist of the wrist in the secondary plane has been deliberately cultivated by some players, who, I believe, hold the opinion that the palm of the hand should face the strings. While at first sight this might seem logical, appearing to have the virtue of 'geometrical tidiness', it disregards several important factors: first, it causes tension by stressing the tendons on the thumb side of the wrist, and constricting those on the opposite side. Second, the tendons which transmit movement from the muscles in the forearm to the fingers are made to pull 'round a corner' instead of directly. Third, with this 'palm-facing' position of the hand, it is the tip of the nail rather than its edge that attacks the string, with consequent loss of tonal quality and depth of sound (see Figs. 7a and b).

Fig. 7a   Fig. 7b

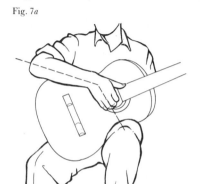
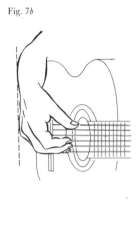

I have developed a three-stage 'drill' for positioning the hand preparatory to playing, which, if followed carefully, avoids unnecessary tension and provides an ideal attitude to the strings for the production of good tone. In stage 1 the forearm is extended in front of the player, with the palm of the hand facing the floor. It is important to check at this stage that there is no sideways bending (secondary movement) of the wrist, and that a straight line could be drawn down the forearm from the elbow to the tip of the middle finger. There must be no lateral deviation of the wrist. In stage 2 the hand drops forward under its own dead weight, allowing the wrist to become limp. The palm should now be facing the elbow and *not* the soundboard of the guitar. The inside of the forearm and the thumb are thus brought almost to a right angle to each other. Stage 3 is the most difficult to describe and also to execute. By rotating the forearm outwards, the wrist is carried away from the guitar to a distance of some 8–10 cm. from its position in stage 2. This movement must take place only from the elbow joint and *not* from the wrist itself. The wrist must not be allowed to twist—remember the straight line from elbow to fingertip in stage 1. In its final position, the palm still faces the elbow and not the soundboard. A 'rule of thumb' guide to the distance of the wrist from the soundboard is that it should be approximately equal to the width at the knuckles of a clenched fist (use the left hand as a gauge).

If all these movements have been carried out correctly, there should be no stress in any part of the body, arms, or hands, with the exception of a very small amount in the right leg due to its slight inward pressure.

Finger action

Before dealing with finger action in detail, I should like to try and dispel some of the confusion which seems to exist over the question of 'plucking' and 'striking' by giving my own definition of each. Plucking implies a movement in which the finger first rests on the string, remains there for a moment, then pulls and releases it. This action consists of three distinct movements: descend—pause—ascend. The finger is propelled in one direction, stopped, and then returned to its original position. This is a somewhat cumbersome and complicated process which contravenes the first physiological principle of the simplest action being likely to be the best. Musically, its effect, when playing repeated notes on one string or arpeggio patterns on several strings, is to emphasize one of the guitar's inherent weaknesses: a general lack of legato and sostenuto characteristics. For the finger to pause on the string—however briefly—must cause a momentary damping of the sound, which destroys continuity. The player whose technique is based on a plucking action will inevitably have great difficulty in playing really smoothly and allowing the music to 'flow'.

The striking action offers much greater resources, both physiologically and tonally. To strike a string suggests that the finger begins its movement some distance from it, accelerates towards it, hits it a glancing blow, and then continues in the same direction; or in other words, it 'follows through'. An analogy with a stroke in tennis or the swing of a golf-club may be used in imagining the action involved. The essential advantages of this method of setting the string in vibration are that (1) only one movement of the finger is needed, in only one direction; (2) the maximum power is generated at the moment of impact, because the finger is still accelerating at this instant instead of slowing down as it does when plucking; and (3) legato playing is made considerably easier, because the contact time between finger and string is reduced to a minimum.

In examining the playing attitude of the fingers, it is still important to retain the feeling of natural movements in the primary and secondary functions of joints and muscles. If the secondary movement (i.e. the finger-spreading action) is largely ignored, it leaves only the primary or gripping action, but since each finger has three joints, an examination of their separate and combined actions is needed so that a clear picture can emerge as to how the finger is propelled towards the string. The strongest and most flexible joint must provide most of the power for the stroke, so obviously the knuckle joint (first phalanx) will be the principle source of this power. (It is perhaps worth noting here that the remaining two phalanges have no secondary movement, and little independence from each other.) The hand is designed chiefly for gripping; attempting to grip an object using only the tip and middle phalanges of the fingers will demonstrate their relative weakness and limited scope of movement. Since these two joints are to play a comparatively small part in the finger's action, it follows that they should remain as free from tension as possible. Another simple experiment will demonstrate this: if the finger is stretched out as straight as it will go, it is obviously tensed; similarly, it is also in a state of tension if it is clenched into the hand. The only attitude it can adopt which leaves it untensed is somewhere between these two extremes, and in which the joints are partially bent. The finger should retain this attitude almost all the time while playing, so that it is able to move as a complete unit from the main joint. (This 'relaxed curve' of the finger needs to be slightly modified in changing from apoyando (supported stroke) to tirando (free stroke) and vice versa, and also when making adjustments from string to string in certain instances.)

A finger action which is based largely on the movement of only one joint will be far more reliable, accurate, and consistent than one which involves two or three joints, since the 'arc' traced by the fingertip will always be the same—like a swinging pendulum. Speed and smoothness of movement will also be much greater. Try bending and straightening the finger rapidly at the middle joint, then compare this with a similar action from the main joint, and notice the difference in strength, fluency, and potential for rapid movement.

Having examined in some detail the action of a single finger in striking a string, it is now necessary to consider the interaction between fingers when alternating or playing sequences of notes. Any sequential action needs to employ what I shall refer to as a 'balanced movement'. This is perhaps best understood by a simple analogy: the weight of the body when walking is transferred alternately from one foot to the other in a smooth, rhythmic motion. The action of the right-hand fingers is very similar: a stroke by one finger coincides with release of pressure by the other. The precise moment at which this 'transfer of weight' occurs is of crucial importance to the development of a perfectly co-ordinated action, as well as to genuine legato playing. The 'resting' finger (apoyando strokes being referred to throughout) must lift from its string at the exact instant—but not a millisecond earlier—that the striking finger sounds the string above. The fingers therefore pass each other at a point between the sounding string and the lower one.

In walking, the feet are only momentarily in simultaneous contact with the ground; they are never both out of contact at the same moment. So with the fingers: the sensation given by the balanced-movement action is one of being in constant contact with the lower string with one or the other finger, while maintaining a smooth, continuous momentum. This contributes greatly to the development of security, reliability, and confidence. The analogy with walking differs in one basic aspect from the balanced movement of right-hand fingers: the fingers are propelled entirely by their own muscles and must not rely on the weight of hand or arm, whereas feet have to bear the body's weight.

The balanced-movement principle applies equally to all right-hand patterns in which single notes are struck in sequence, whether of scale or arpeggio form, by two or three fingers, using any number of strings in any grouping.

Tone production

Having discussed the purely physiological aspects of right-hand finger action, it is now necessary to see how these relate to the task of setting the guitar strings in motion effectively.

A dynamic right-hand attack depends, in essence, on one fundamental principle: if a string is struck inwards towards the body of the guitar, it will produce a louder and fuller sound than if it is pulled away from it (plucking action) or merely deflected sideways in a line parallel to the soundboard. The truth of this statement can easily be checked by scientific measurement, but for our purposes another simple experiment is all that is needed. A single stroke from the index finger directed inwards on to any open string, bringing the finger to rest against the next lower string (apoyando), will at once demonstrate how much fuller and more resonant this note is than even the most vigorous pluck of the string away from the guitar. From the point of view of technical development, striking flexes the finger muscles to their fullest extent if practised firmly and regularly. The strength of these muscles is thereby gradually increased until a point is reached where there is ample power available to produce even the loudest note of which the guitar is capable. The plucking action, apart from producing a generally thinner, weaker tone, is likely to cause the string to slap against the fingerboard with an unmusical rattle, whether it is pulled outwards or just sideways.

With the hand positioned as described, and with pendulum-like strokes of the finger from its main joint, the most efficient attack, the principal direction of which is inwards, can be achieved. Thus, both physiological and tonal requirements are satisfied.

The next point is the extent or length of the stroke. Since the striking action requires the finger to start its movement *off* the string, careful thought is needed as to the exact distance from the string at which the stroke must begin. As one of the main objectives of this backlift is to allow the finger to generate momentum by accelerating up to the moment of impact, it might seem that the further away it begins the better. However, an exaggeratedly long backlift is impractical, because (1) the greater the distance the finger has to travel towards its target (i.e. the string), the less likely it is to hit it with any precision—or indeed at all!—and (2) the longer the journey, the more time is taken, thus limiting speed of execution. Economy of movement and effort requires a minimum backlift, but the stroke must nevertheless be capable of producing maximum tone. Of course, it is always possible to strike the strings of any guitar with such force that they will rattle or buzz, so obviously the attack must be just below this level— that is to say, maximum volume consistent with pure tone. Experience shows that this can be achieved with a backlift of no more than about 0.5 cm. The object here is simply to define the upper limit of volume, but it goes without saying that the guitar is capable of graded dynamics downwards to *ppp* or even less. It must always be borne in mind that the direction of movement of the fingers is towards the hand, or along the line of the arm, rather than at right angles to the strings.

Although the foregoing remarks are intended to show the efficient use of the right-hand fingers in playing apoyando, it should not be thought that this is only of use in a specialized way—for example, for playing scales, accented notes, melodic lines, etc. It should be seen as an indispensable exercise for the development of strength and positive attack in the right-hand fingers. It is therefore of great importance that a high proportion of purely technical practising-time should be devoted to apoyando playing.

The firmness and certainty which is gained in this way is just as necessary for the correct execution of tirando, to which the same basic principles apply. The action of the finger must be identical for both types of stroke in the approach to the string and at the moment of impact; more especially, there must be no element of plucking when using the tirando stroke. The only real difference from apoyando occurs *after* the contact between finger and string, when a very slight deflection of the tip joint takes place in order to allow the finger to clear the lower string. This clearance needs to be no more than 1 mm. Such precise finger control calls for much practising; eventually the sound produced by the two types of stroke should be virtually indistinguishable.

Very attentive readers may have noticed what appears to be inconsistency in the above description of right-hand finger action. Having said that the finger is propelled chiefly by the muscle which activates the main joint, I have now advocated a movement of the *tip* joint as part of the mechanics of the tirando stroke. There is no inconsistency here, since this is merely an example of a secondary joint being used for a secondary purpose. The tip is only being employed in a passive role—taking 'avoiding action'—while the power for the stroke is still provided entirely by the main joint.

Another example of how the tip and middle joints have their respective roles to play in the overall pattern of right-hand technique can be seen in the differing attitudes which the fingers need to adopt for scale-type passages as compared to arpeggio patterns. (The latter category includes chord-playing, since the basic finger dispositions are the same.) If all the fingers are placed on one string, the tip and middle joints will need to be bent to varying degrees for each finger (because of their unequal lengths). Now, placing one finger on each of the three treble strings (as for a simple arpeggio), a different degree of bend is needed in the first and third fingers; only the second finger will remain approximately as before. The first has to bend a little more, while the third straightens slightly. Experienced players make these adjustments subconsciously.

Digressing for a moment: this 'finger-bend adjustment' provides an example of how general technical principles have occasionally to be modified slightly from player to player. Some people have a ring-finger which is longer than the index, some the opposite, and yet others have these two fingers of equal length. Whatever curvature is necessary to ensure confident contact with the strings (without alteration of the hand position, of course), this will be the attitude which the finger must adopt and maintain all the time in playing on any string.

Since motive power is being supplied by the main joint, it is not necessary in any case for the tip and middle joints to alter their relative positions during the execution of the stroke—with the exception of the small tip movement described above in relation to the free stroke.

So as to maintain consistency in both finger action and angle of attack whichever string is being struck, the arm and hand, moving as a unit, must traverse the strings in an arc, pivoting from the arm's resting-point on the edge of the guitar. If the arm is balanced, as already described, movement through this arc will require minimal effort, and, if correctly executed, will not cause any alteration in the relative positions of hand, wrist, and arm. If the arm is not perfectly balanced at its resting-point, or if its movement is not symmetrical, the alignment of the hand to the strings will be disturbed, and there will be a tendency to try and compensate for this by adjusting the middle and tip joints of the fingers. When ascending from bass to treble, they will tend to 'reach out' for the next higher string by straightening at the middle joint. In descending from treble to bass, they will tend to retract into the hand by increasing the bend in this joint. In the latter case, a plucking action is likely to be substituted for the correct stroke. In cases where control of the arm movement is really poor, there is a risk of the wrist becoming involved, which, by bending it further, causes tension and strain.

Using the thumb as a 'crutch' on a lower string, or on the end of the fingerboard, is also seriously inhibiting to the free movement of the arm, and will almost certainly cause faulty finger adjustment. This habit, which probably originated with flamenco players, strongly suggests that the arm is incorrectly balanced and lacking in stability. It is to be avoided at all times.

As a general technical principle, the whole finger must move as a single unit in a 'swinging', pendulum-like action towards the string, without significant alteration to the natural bend of middle and tip joints. Technical faults such as those described above should be detected quickly and corrected before they become habitual. They are the cause of much unreliable finger action and uneven tone production.

Crossing the strings by pivoting the arm from its resting-point on the guitar is an essential function in playing scale-type passages, where the distance traversed by the fingertips is approximately 5 cm.—from the bottom string to the top. This movement is no less necessary, though possibly more subtle in execution, when the texture of the music is in arpeggio form. Examples 1 and 2, from studies by Aguado and Villa-Lobos, illustrate the grouping of fingers on strings, and the shifting of the arm which is needed.

Ex. 1. Aguado *Study No. 8*

Ex. 2. Villa-Lobos *Étude No. 1*

Reproduced by permission of Editions Max Eschig, Paris/United Music Publishers Ltd.

It may not have escaped the notice of the keen student that, as the arm carries the hand across the strings, it also produces a slight movement along them towards the bridge. Logically, this would have the effect of causing the sound to be more ponticello on the treble strings than on the bass. However, this is more theoretical than practical, because what might be termed 'tonal definition' is much less marked on the bass strings; the ear is more sensitive to changes of tone colour in the upper register. A very slight change in tone colour would in any case be a small price to pay for the greatly enhanced technical security of this kind of arm movement, which, by its smoothness of action, makes the graduation of tone so small as to be virtually undetectable. The fingers must in any case learn to compensate for the audibly differing characteristics of the strings themselves. In other words, the tone colour of ① will always be 'thinner' than that of ②, which will in turn be thinner than that of ③. Try striking ① and then ③ with the same finger, and note the marked difference between them.

Any attempt to define 'good' tone, and to explain how to produce it, is bound to be controversial; for example, the argument about whether nail or flesh sound is to be preferred stretches back into history. Yet during the last half-century or so it seems to have been resolved quite decisively in favour of nails. The reasons for this, now that we know the outcome, are worth stating. The nail is capable of producing a louder note, a wider range of tone colour, and, above all, far greater clarity of attack. The nail method has therefore been universally adopted by players with professional aspirations, as well as by amateurs who hope to emulate them.

This, then, would seem to clinch the argument, though there is still some residual support for the use of nail *and* flesh in combination. It is difficult to follow the somewhat obscure logic of this theory. One wonders whether some kind of nostalgic conservatism prevents a clean break with the past; or could it be that excessive timidity creates a feeling that to rely on something as thin and fragile as the unsupported nail invites technical insecurity to the point of incoherence? Whatever the reason, the method itself (combined nail and flesh) is unsound, since clarity and legato are sacrificed, and extraneous noise is increased. If the action of a finger were seen in slow motion, it would be easy to detect the disadvantages which are inseparable from the nail/flesh type of attack. If the finger begins its stroke at about 0.5 cm. above the string, the first point of contact is between string and *flesh*. The fingertip then continues across the string until contact is made between *nail* and string. There are several undesirable results from this. First, a slight scraping sound is produced by the friction of flesh on string. Secondly, the string is momentarily damped, and prevented from vibrating during the moment of flesh contact. This results in a brief silence between one note and the next—an involuntary staccato. Further, unwanted noise in the form of a slight 'click' may occur as the string passes from fingertip to nail.

These are the main disadvantages of the nail/flesh attack,

and while they may seem relatively unimportant, a comparison with the tone produced by a good 'nail-only' player will show the marked superiority of the latter in clarity and legato. Nail-only playing is possibly marginally more demanding in terms of sheer precision, but this is only a matter of practice.

Speed of execution is likely to be impaired by a nail/flesh attack, the only advantage of which (so I have read) is that: 'something of the softness of flesh tone remains in the note after the nail has left the string' (*sic!*). I should have thought that until the string has been released by the last surface with which it was in contact (i.e. the nail), no sound at all can be produced! What happens to the string before it is set in vibration can have no bearing at all—for good or ill—on the final sound, since all the time that the flesh is in contact with it, the string is motionless.

I believe the uncompromising truth to be that nails, and nails alone, should be used. If the player is unfortunate enough to suffer from poor nail growth, he will have to put up with flesh sound—a poor substitute, but one that can be partly mitigated if enough practising is done to encourage the fingertips to harden, as do those of the left hand.

Now to the main question of tone production. When discussing something as subjective as tone quality, the first problem arises from the need to define what is meant by 'good' tone as distinct from 'bad' or 'mediocre'. This definition is particularly difficult to formulate in words only, without aural illustrations. One is tempted to avoid the issue altogether, and simply to describe the technical aspects of how the sound is produced. Even this limited objective would not be without its difficulties, for it must be remembered that any theoretical approach is capable of being applied in a variety of ways, and its application is, to some extent, dependent on the natural physical characteristics of the player, and on the shape and condition of his nails. (This should not, however, be used as an excuse for a sloppy approach to technique; personal idiosyncrasies are one thing, but sound basic principles are immutable!)

Perhaps a better way to tackle the subject would be by a process of elimination—by identifying all the undesirable features of a poor sound. The guitar tends to suffer more than most instruments from extraneous noises such as clicks, squeaks, rattles, buzzes, and muffled notes. These are more noticeable than they would be on most other instruments, due to the relatively limited dynamic range of the guitar. The fact that they occur at all is to some extent an indication of imperfect technical control. (The whistle which is made by a finger sliding along a wire-covered bass string is an exception; it seems to be practically unavoidable, given the present fairly crude state of string-making technology, which has scarcely changed in 300 years.)

The avoidance of 'action noise', or non-musical sounds, is the first requirement of good tone production. Many hours of really concentrated and painstaking practising will be needed to develop the standard of cleanness in playing of the world's best guitarists. As a first step, a very careful examination of all the causes of the unwanted noises must be undertaken. Some of these are due to faulty left-hand technique, others to right-hand defects, and yet others to poor co-ordination between the two hands.

The second requirement, clarity of attack, is closely connected with freedom from extraneous noises, but there is another quality, which might be called 'incisive articulation', which is a very desirable feature of guitar tone. A cleanly struck note will give more 'bite' to the rhythm, will have longer duration, and will project much more positively. Achieving consistent clarity means paying very careful attention to detail in the approach of the finger to the string; contact must be made at precisely the right point on the nail, and at the correct angle. Over a fairly long period, confidence and certainty will develop. Any trace of hesitancy in the approach of the finger to the string will slow it down, diminishing and diffusing the sound at the moment of impact. Being able to strike the strings with confidence is fundamental to a secure technique, and stems from the knowledge that one's method is basically sound, and also from a determination to be positive, even when mistakes are made.

The third requirement of good tone is an absence of 'thinness' or 'tinniness'. These are not very precise terms, but anyone who has played the guitar using nails knows what they mean. Acoustically, a 'tinny'-sounding note has a higher proportion of upper partial harmonics in its composition. Some players (and listeners) imagine that this kind of sound is inseparable from nail tone. That this is not the case can be shown by first striking with the nail parallel to the string (thin sound), and then at an angle of about forty-five degrees to it, drawing the nail across it diagonally. In the latter instance, a much fuller and rounder sound is produced.

An objection which might be raised here is that ponticello tone, which is a legitimate effect on the guitar, has this 'thinner', or brighter, quality of sound; but normal tone cannot be equated with deliberately played ponticello, unvarying use of which would be very tiring to the listener's ear. Basic tone needs to be full and round as well as clear; while any beginner will produce a thin, weak tone, careful cultivation of the 'rounded' quality is necessary. It could perhaps be argued that a method of tone production which gives an unrelieved 'tasto' quality could be just as tiresome to the listener as the strident jangle of thin tone, but this is not entirely true, and in any case a full, round sound provides a much better starting-point as it embodies all the basic mechanics from which a wide spectrum of tone colour—including ponticello—can be developed.

The fourth requirement is what I can only describe as 'body' or depth of tone. If a string is pulled upwards, away from the guitar, then quite apart from the string-rattle caused, the tone will be found to lack 'weight'. In contrast, a note sounded by a firm apoyando stroke directed inwards at the guitar body will have 'punch' and depth. For the cultivation of this quality of tone, I recommend much practising of apoyando, even in patterns such as arpeggios or tremolo which would normally be played tirando. This provides vital training for a positive attack by the fingers, and establishes habits which will still produce a firm tone when tirando is being used., In these circumstances, apoyando is being employed as a practising device, and may or may not be used in arpeggio-playing in performance.

To sum up: a technically sound right-hand method must satisfy two separate sets of criteria—physiological and tonal—and these must obviously be fully compatible. The physiological factors are:

1 Use of primary muscles and joints in their most natural modes, and independently of all muscles and joints which are not directly involved in playing

2 Training of finger muscles to a greater degree of strength than is actually required. This gives a feeling of ease and fluency to the playing of even the most strenuous passage, as well as developing complete control over all aspects of tone and volume

3 Economy of movement and effort

The tonal factors are:

1 Cleanness
2 Clarity, or purity of tone
3 'Roundness', or warmth of timbre
4 Depth, or weight of tone

All that remains now is to examine the technical means by which these criteria can be met. The main requirements of cleanness and clarity are speed (of finger movement), and accuracy of attack—and of course, much practising. Roundness and depth of tone depend mainly on angle and direction of attack. Several angles are involved in fact, but at least two of these are governed by the position of the forearm on the guitar edge, which ensures its alignment at an angle of approximately forty-five degrees to the strings. When moving along the line of the arm, the fingers will approach the string diagonally, and contact will be made on the left side of the nail. Although this is an essential element in the production of a full, round tone, it does not guarantee it, since it would still be possible to pull or hook the string upwards. Another vital angle is best seen by looking along the fingerboard from the 'nut' end. From this viewpoint, the tip joint of the finger should appear to be almost perpendicular to the soundboard at the moment of contact. It is this attitude of finger to string which causes the inward pressure mentioned earlier, and which gives weight and depth to the sound. One further angle needs considering—although it is largely dictated by the others—and is best seen by the player, sitting normally but moving his head a little to the right, so viewing the fingers from directly above. The inside of the tip joint of the *i* finger should now appear to be forty-five degrees to the string, that of the *m* finger at a slightly more obtuse angle, and the *a* finger at a more obtuse angle still. Care should be taken to see that the *a* finger is not absolutely 'square on' at ninety degrees to the string if thin tone is to be avoided; a small adjustment of the forearm to bring the wrist inwards may be necessary. The actual point on the nail at which the initial contact with the string is made is generally about 0.5 cm. down from its tip, on the left side, though this will vary a little with nail shape. This point of contact must be on the under-side of the nail edge—a most important condition of good tone. After meeting the string at this point, the string in effect slides obliquely along the nail a small distance as the finger moves inwards towards the hand, then leaves it at a point about 0.25 cm. closer to the tip. If the edge and under-surface of the nail have been carefully prepared, and provided that the finger movement is towards the hand ('along the line of the arm'), there will be little friction. Contact time, and therefore staccato and extraneous noise, will be reduced to a minimum.

The thumb

All instruments have their limitations—the guitar perhaps more than its fair share. One of the more obvious is its lack of volume and carrying power, though recent improvements in design and construction, together with developments in play-ing techniques, have at least partially redressed the balance with orchestral and keyboard instruments.

Balance, in another sense, is a common weakness in much guitar-playing, and one which has received surprisingly little attention. The guitar is, for want of a better description, a 'self-accompanying' instrument like the piano. Dynamic even-ness throughout its range is therefore an essential quality which should be built in to the instrument itself, as well as being a part of the player's normal technical equipment; yet most guitars are prone to excessive bass resonance compared to their treble. Part of the problem may perhaps be due to the different response of metal-covered bass strings and nylon monofilament trebles, though the chief cause must surely be the size and shape of the guitar's 'sounding-box' relative to its normal frequency range. There is still scope for makers to modify the traditional 'Spanish' sound of a 'booming' bass and 'boxy' treble, thereby improving the overall balance.

This general tonal imbalance is often reinforced by the player's over-energetic or clumsy and ill-coordinated thumb technique. Since the thumb is unarguably the hand's strongest digit, it is capable of a much more forceful stroke than the fingers. This is accentuated still more if the thumb has not been trained to move from its main joint, in its primary mode, without bending at the tip or middle joints and without any assistance from the forearm. If the arm is allowed to propel the thumb, its weight, assisted by gravity, adds still further to the strength of the attack on already over-resonant bass strings.

Very sparing use should be made by the thumb of apoyando strokes. It is clear that this kind of attack emphasizes the bass at the expense of the treble still more. There are seldom compelling reasons for the use of thumb apoyando, though occasionally a particular passage, such as an unaccompanied bass melody, may be more effective played in this way. Apart from tone and balance, there are physiological reasons for the thumb's training to be largely in tirando strokes.

As with the fingers, the thumb strikes the string using its primary movement, though a small amount of secondary movement is needed on the return journey. The backlift begins by the thumb moving straight back from its main joint (the other two joints being kept straight) until the nail is about 0.5 cm. beyond the string it is aiming to strike. It then descends, still being kept straight and moving only from the main joint, hitting the string on the left side of the nail and continuing on towards the hand; its action may then be checked by the middle joint of the index finger, though this is not necessarily invariably the case. The whole action, from the stroke's beginning until the thumb returns to its starting-point, traces a long, narrow oval path in which the secondary movement is used only for avoiding-action on the return journey. This it does by means of a very slight lateral movement outwards of no more than 0.5 cm. as it passes the strings.

Because of its position on the hand in relation to the guitar's strings, the thumb is inclined to move across them in a 'surface' motion instead of applying the slight inward pressure which has been described in the observations on tone. It is just as important for the thumb, as for the fingers, to cultivate an attack in which this inward pressure is applied to the string at the moment of impact, but careful control is needed if an unintentional 'bass-heavy' technique is not to become a habit. Where apoyando is to be used, a slight displacement of the wrist and forearm is needed; if they are held in their normal position, the thumb will miss the adjacent string by a few millimetres. This displacement takes the form of a (minimal) movement outwards (away from the guitar) of the wrist.

Geometrically, the thumb's motion is of a radius (measured from main joint to nail tip) moving through an arc. When (for example) the bottom—E—string is struck tirando, the fifth—A—string is avoided because the thumb is then moving not only downwards but outwards as well. If apoyando is used, the wrist needs to be further away from the strings so that the arc traced by the nail tip's trajectory bisects both E and A strings. This realignment of the hand affects not only the thumb, but the fingers' action too, as the changed angle of attack tends to cause them to pluck rather than to strike the strings.

One further point can be made about the bass-heavy tendency of guitars and guitarists' techniques. Due to overtones, the instrument's bottom register is inclined to sound more diffuse and 'muddy' than the upper range. The importance of clarity and balance throughout the compass has already been stressed, and to avoid adding to existing problems, the thumb needs to be trained with far more careful attention than is usual for guitarists.

In the section on finger action, I referred to the need for a 'balanced movement' when fingers play in alternation or in sequence. The same principle applies to the thumb when it is incorporated into a pattern with fingers. For example: in the sequence *p*, *i*, *m*, *a*, played on the bottom string and the top three, the *i* finger lifts preparatory to striking simultaneously with the thumb's impact, the *p* lifts whilst *i* strikes, and so on. This simple example shows only one of many possible finger/thumb patterns, all of which should conform to the balanced-movement principle.

Some right-hand faults

The complexity and subtlety of right-hand technique make it impossible to list all the faults which are likely to develop; some of these are due to a misunderstanding or misinterpretation of the principles involved, and others to inattention or lack of awareness in practising. However, I shall attempt to analyse two of the commonest technical errors.

A theory which could be described as showing an imperfect understanding of the mechanics and physiology of right-hand finger action is that the tip joint should give way or 'flex' on contacting the string, either by straightening or even bending backwards. The advantage claimed for this action is that it produces a 'softer' sound, though it is not clear whether this term applies to volume, timbre, or both. It certainly produces a quieter and less clear note—rather like flesh tone—but this is due simply to mechanical inefficiency. A given amount of energy having been generated by the main joint's muscle, the tip joint, by acting as a 'shock absorber', then reduces the energy to be transmitted to the string to perhaps only half the amount. Momentary damping and therefore slight staccato also occurs due to the longer contact time between nail and string while the tip joint is flexing.

A more efficient way of varying the volume is to control the amount of power applied by the main joint in the first instance, and to vary tone quality by controlled use of apoyando and tirando, tasto and ponticello, but retaining the 'relaxed-curve' attitude of the finger throughout the action. In the same way as ponticello and tasto can represent many shades of timbre as well as the extremes, so also the attack can be graduated through a whole range of dynamics from apoyando ff down to tirando pp. Such fine control of right-hand fingers, which should be part of every guitarist's technical armoury, requires many hours of painstaking practising.

Another fault, which often appears to the observer to be more of a mannerism than a technical device, is the tendency of the hand (and sometimes the arm too) to move leftwards as the finger strikes the string; the power for the stroke therefore seems to come from the arm rather than from the finger. This faulty action, which is deliberately cultivated by some players (*sic!*), appears to stem from a mistaken belief that it is the only way in which the 'round' sound described earlier can be produced. The problem arises through confusion over the difference between playing on the side of the nail and moving the finger sideways. Reduced speed of execution and unreliability are only two of the penalties to be paid for use of this eccentric action.

Damping

The sonority of guitar music has come to be associated with much holding of notes beyond their written values, and many resonances which the composer may not have intended, particularly where open strings are involved. It can be argued, and often is, that this 'harmonic' quality is inseparable from, and is indeed part of, the charm of the instrument. There is a certain amount of truth in this, but the fact remains that contemporary composers and arrangers are becoming more fastidious in their insistence on strict observance of written note values. Notes which are intended to continue sounding for their natural duration are increasingly being indicated by the addition of an 'open-ended' tie-line. Elsewhere it is expected that some form of damping technique will be employed. Harpists, who have much the same problem, have always regarded damping as an integral part of technical training.

Several effective methods for damping unwanted resonances exist on the guitar—some using the right hand and some the left, depending on which hand is least occupied at any moment. Open bass strings, which are the most troublesome, can almost always be damped by light pressure from the flesh of the thumb. Should the thumb be needed to strike another string immediately, damping can be left until after this second string has been struck, for example: (1) Strike string ⑥; (2) Strike string ⑤; (3) Damp string ⑥. This method is both neat and effective and can be used with any combination of bass strings, open or stopped. Damping more than one string simultaneously is easily done by a disengaged left-hand finger, but if the right hand must be used, a small inward displacement of the wrist and slight bending of the tip joint will allow the side of the thumb to be brought into light contact with all three strings at once.

The method of damping treble strings is by straightforward contact with the flesh of the fingers, and is too obvious to need detailed description.

Lastly, all six strings may be damped after playing a full chord by momentarily straightening the wrist and using either the side of a straight thumb or the palm of the hand.

Chords

Many teachers of the guitar introduce the playing of double notes and chords much too early in the student's course of study. For musical as well as technical reasons, the guitarist ought to be thoroughly familiar with, and fluent in, single-note playing in all registers of the instrument (having also developed a strong feeling for 'line') before tackling the problems of polyphonic and harmonic textures. In a perfect world this would always be the case, but the ever-present temptation to play music which is too advanced for the technical stage which has been reached often proves too great to resist. As a result, much wooden, jerky, and unmusical phrasing is heard, mostly due to a tendency to think 'vertically' when performing pieces written in two or more voices. The technical difficulties of rhythmic co-ordination, legato, dynamic balance, and continuity in several voices at once present formidable hurdles. Many hours of preparation by way of single-line practising would go far in smoothing the path. It is not without reason that teachers of *all* instruments have for centuries advocated the practising of scales; they are the bedrock of a controlled technique. In a later chapter, when methods of practising are examined (Chap. 8), it will become even clearer why so much emphasis is given to the practising of monophonic textures.

A chord is, by definition, three or more notes played simultaneously. A double note, though not strictly a chord, can often give a full harmonic impression on the guitar because of sympathetic resonances and overtones, especially when an open string forms one of the notes of the implied chord—so long as the attack is precise and balanced. The illusion of complete harmony can easily be destroyed when playing a double note, especially with thumb and finger, if the disparate strengths of these digits is not borne in mind; even more so if the parts are rhythmically separated as they are in Example 3.

Ex. 3

Apart from the harmonic aspect, two parts should, almost without exception, be kept exactly together to avoid giving an impression of sloppy and unrhythmical playing. If the lower note is played on the beat, splitting the parts will cause the upper note to be late; if the upper note is on the beat, then the lower note must be early. Lack of technical control—the cause of part-separation—is almost always due to allowing the thumb to be propelled by the arm's weight instead of by its own muscle. Even a very small downward movement of the hand when playing the bass note must cause a delay, as the hand must then return to its position before the finger can play. The best cure for this fault is to practise a light tirando attack with the thumb, and a firmer apoyando stroke with the finger. The sensation to aim for is one in which the weight of the attack seems to be more behind the finger than the thumb. Not only must the two parts be played exactly together rhythmically, but for a musical result they must also be precisely matched in tone and volume. The observations on thumb technique should be carefully noted.

Keeping two parts together is a rule that should (with rare exceptions) be observed at all times. More flexibility is possible in the case of three-, four-, five-, and six-note chords. Guitarists have a tendency to overuse the 'spread' or 'arpeggiated' chord, which can only diminish its effectiveness—like eating caviare for every meal! As with many other guitaristic habits, a preference is thus revealed for the technically easy, comfortable, or convenient; for technical 'shadow' rather than musical substance!

While the spread chord is a perfectly legitimate and very beautiful effect, it is possible on only a few instruments, notably the guitar, the harp, and the piano. It is therefore a useful, though not essential, tool of musical expression. One positive effect of its use which is often overlooked by guitarists is that it creates an accent on whichever beat it occurs; it ought therefore to be restricted to those points in the music which actually need such emphasis; for example, the first beats of bars, syncopated accents, climactic notes, final notes of phrases, etc. Such sparing and controlled use will have more impact and will enhance the music far more than indiscriminate or 'technically convenient' spreading.

When the melody note is at the top of the chord—its usual place—it is generally played on the beat, with the rest of the chord sounding just before it. To give a feeling of climax when the top note is reached, there needs to be a slight crescendo in the arpeggiation from bottom to top; this is another reason for keeping the bass note fairly subdued.

Bass melodies are not uncommon in guitar music, and the bottom note of a chord can be given slight emphasis by detaching it from the rest of the chord, which may then be played either spread or together. It is hardly ever advisable to accent a bass note with thumb apoyando unless the melody is very slow and the texture of the music gives ample time for the hand to readjust for the finger-played part of the chord after each melody note.

More unusually, the principal melodic interest can be in an inner voice. The most effective way of playing Examples 4 and

Ex. 4. Albeniz *Granada*

Ex. 5. De Falla *Hommage a Debussy*

Ex. 6. De Falla *Hommage à Debussy*

Reproduced by kind permission of J. & W. Chester Ltd.

5 is first to spread the whole chord, then rapidly to replay the melodic note with the thumb. Even more rare is the chord in which the melodic note is almost, but not quite, at the top (see Example 6): this precludes the use of the thumb as in Examples 4 and 5. The technique here is to spread the chord, but with fingers playing in the order *p*, *i*, *a*, *m*. The important note may be given a slight accent by playing *m* apoyando.

Chords of five or six notes are almost always spread. The thumb glides over the bass strings, for which the arc of movement requires the wrist to drop slightly and then recover rapidly to complete the chord by the fingers playing one each of the top three strings. To achieve a musical result, great care must be taken to see that all the notes are evenly spaced rhythmically; evenness rather than speed is the important factor. An alternative method of playing these fuller chords is to glide the thumb across all the strings with a 'brushing' action from a loosely held wrist, like running a stick along a railing. A gentle beginning with a very slight increase in pressure as the thumb crosses the strings will ensure the crescendo towards the top note.

Ex. 7

Composers (or arrangers) who do not know the guitar well sometimes write a five-part chord from which an inner string is omitted (see Example 7). This clearly precludes the 'thumb-only' method unless some form of left-hand damping of the unwanted string is employed. Even the 'thumb and fingers' attack can be awkward and produce a 'lumpy' and uneven sound. The solution is often to rearrange or respace the chord, adding or omitting a note according to context. Five-part chords always present something of a problem, even when the notes lie on five adjacent strings, mainly because the thumb finds it easier to glide over three strings than only two. It needs to be particularly well controlled to keep the spreading of the notes rhythmically even.

Chords with unusual spacings—whether of four, five, or six notes—occur quite often in music which was originally written for the lute. Understanding why the composer chose a particular spacing in the first place is essential in deciding whether, and in what way, to modify it. Example 8 shows one of many such chords to be found in lute music. With the lute's different tuning, the three lower notes of this chord are played as open strings, and only the top note, D, has to be

Ex. 8

stopped by the left hand (at the seventh fret). Obviously, ease of left-hand fingering has taken precedence over right-hand facility. The benefit of easy left-hand fingering no longer exists when the chord is played on the guitar, and there is therefore no technical advantage to be gained in trying to reproduce the original spacing exactly. Musical reasons, such as continuity of part-writing in the inner voices, could, but need not, prevent respacing; otherwise, the arrangement of the chord in Example 9 is much more comfortable for the right hand, and has a more guitaristic sound, but does not place any undue burden on the left hand. Another possible solution is to omit the fifth of the chord (A) altogether. This might be regarded as a last resort, but could nevertheless be done without seriously impairing the harmony.

Assuming that the chord must, for whatever reason, be left in its original form, the only remaining technical solution must

Ex. 9

be to make a special study of odd string/finger combinations[1] and to practise them carefully. As well as helping to solve any immediate problem, this will add another facet of right-hand control to the player's technical armoury.

Although I have said that five- and six-note chords need always to be spread, it is possible to play them with a percuss ive attack of the thumb which almost gives the impression of a single sound, though of necessity such chords will occur at places in the music where forte, fortissimo, or sforzando are called for. One further technique of playing these chords is the flamenco player's *rasgueado* (literally, 'rasping'!), wherein the backs of the nails are drawn across the strings; this too can sound quite integrated if executed with confidence.

The action of right-hand fingers and thumb is, and should always be, the same mechanically, whether playing individually as in single-note passages, or collectively as in chord-playing. Use of apoyando strokes is of course restricted, but even these can be employed in certain selected instances.

The most usual fault in performing a chord is for the fingers to be placed on the strings in preparation. The arguments against this practice apply equally to single-note and chord-playing: plucking action instead of striking; momentary damping of strings; use of secondary joint movements; lack of positive attack due to the absence of an accelerating approach to the string. The cause of this defective action is most likely to be uncertainty on the part of the fingers as to the precise location of the strings, and this in turn is most probably due to instability of the hand and arm. The effect is that the fingers need to 'feel for the strings' before playing them. That such an action, with its disastrous effect on smooth articulation and dynamic balance, can still be advocated by some teachers and writers is more than just surprising.

The correct and only logical method of playing a chord (without arpeggiation) is for the fingers and thumb to approach the strings as a group from the usual distance of 0.5 cm., then to strike and follow through without pausing on the

---

[1] See Study No. 6 in S. Dodgson and H. Quine, *Ten Studies for Guitar* (London, 1965).

strings—the whole action from start to finish to be in one continuous movement. If the chord is to be arpeggiated, this procedure needs to be varied slightly: on making contact with the strings, the thumb continues without pausing; *i* follows almost immediately—having been in contact with its string for only the briefest fraction of a second—then *m* for a fraction longer, and finally *a*. The whole action, if performed smoothly, should give the sensation of having been executed in one continuous movement. This requires precise co-ordination and control. It also needs confidence; a tentative or cautious approach will never achieve the desired result.

Ex. 10   Ex. 11   Ex. 12   Ex. 13

A four-stage 'practising programme' provides the best and most effective way of developing the necessary control (see Examples 10–13): In stage 1 the chord is played as a normal arpeggio—thumb tirando, fingers apoyando. Careful attention must be paid to evenness in volume, tone, and rhythm, and also to balance between thumb and fingers, as this stage sets the standard for what follows. Stage 2 is identical, except that the fingers now play tirando. When compared with stage 1, tone and volume should show barely any difference. Stage 3 consists of a slow, evenly spread chord, in which fingers and thumb approach the strings simultaneously but continue their strokes in sequence. Put more plainly, they all contact their strings at the same moment and 'peel off' in turn without pausing. Again, comparison with stages 1 and 2 should show no difference in tone or volume. There must be no spreading or arpeggiation of the chord in stage 4; all fingers and the thumb approach, attack, and follow through in one uninterrupted action. Tone, volume, and balance must be consistent with the three earlier stages; this is checked by immediately returning to stage 1 for comparison.

Like most other aspects of technical mastery, complete control of chord-playing will need practising many times. The above sequential routine is the best way of achieving this. At a later stage this may be combined with the four-stage chord sequence for the left hand (p. 58 below),[1] but to begin with, patient work with each hand separately will be beneficial.

[1] This may be supplemented with Study No. 6 in S. Dodgson and H. Quine, *Twelve Introductory Studies* (London, 1986).

5

LEFT ARM AND HAND

THE right hand may be considered as the *artist* in guitar-playing, and the left as the *artisan* whose work consists almost entirely of preparing notes for articulation by the right hand. Though the functions of the hands are so different, the same physiological principles govern the operation of both. The right arm's weight is supported by the guitar, while the left arm appears to have to support itself through tension in the biceps muscle. Although this is partly true, if, with shoulder and upper arm held loosely, the forearm is raised from the elbow and the thumb is allowed to lean against the guitar neck, some support is gained. If the wrist is also allowed to relax, the hand is brought forward in front of the fingerboard—where it needs to be—and pressure of the thumb in opposition to the fingers can be clearly felt; the arm is also prevented from pulling backwards.

The thumb is both a focal point and a counterbalancing force to the fingers' actions, but to avoid unnecessary tension, and to discourage pulling by the arm, it must remain fully extended, never bending at any joint.[1] Its point of contact with the guitar must be in the lower half of the neck.

A left-hand principle which is not always understood is that all pressure on the strings must be by means of a gripping action, and not by 'arm pull'. 'Gripping' implies, and does in fact mean, equal pressure from thumb and fingers in direct opposition to each other. If this fact is constantly borne in mind when practising, tension in arm, wrist, and hand will be substantially reduced, and endurance correspondingly increased. A useful tip is always to let the elbow fall to the lowest point allowed by finger alignment on the strings. Pressure should ideally be applied to the fingerboard at right angles (see Fig. 8). If the arm pulls backwards, this line becomes dis-

[1] Some thumbs are able to bend backwards at the tip. If this seems natural, it should not be artificially prevented from happening.

Fig. 8

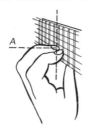

torted, and the stronger the pull, the greater the degree of misalignment and the less direct the pressure on the strings.

To understand fully the complex physiological problems posed by left-hand technique, the various roles of the thumb need to be studied closely. In addition to helping to support the arm and providing a counterweight to pressure from the fingers, the thumb is also the focus and pivot for hand, wrist, and arm movements in two planes, and acts as the base from which all finger actions originate. Its positioning and use are therefore critical to the development of an efficient technique.

The design of the hand is not ideal for guitar-playing; the thumb in particular would balance the four fingers much better if it were attached to the centre of the hand instead of to the side. This immutable anatomical fact of life is basically why the third and fourth fingers are much less developed than the first and second, which, opposing the thumb as they do, have been constantly exercised in everyday life by the action of gripping, whereas the third and fourth have been neglected by comparison. The demands of guitar-playing require the four fingers to be as nearly as possible equal in strength, and this strength is more likely to develop in the third and fourth fingers if the thumb is so positioned as to oppose them. (Four thumbs—one for each finger—would be ideal!) By making use of the main joint's secondary movement, it is possible, without undue strain, to bring the thumb across the palm of the hand until it is opposite the second finger; or even, depending on individual flexibility, to a point between the second and third fingers. While still slightly favouring the first and second fingers, the thumb will now be found to give more support to the third and fourth fingers than if it were allowed to remain opposite the first, or outside the fingers' span; only when the fingers are stopping notes above the twelfth fret should the thumb be permitted to stray beyond the line of the index finger.

If the design of the thumb is not exactly ideal for guitar-playing, neither do the fingers meet the perfect specification; their differing lengths and strengths call for many adjustments and compromises. This can be achieved more efficiently and effortlessly with systematic planning. Extensive use needs to be made of both primary and secondary movements, often in combination. Fingers must conform to three basic rules if clean and clear tone production is to be achieved consistently:

1 Fingertips must be right behind, but not overlapping, the frets
2 Tip joints must stand as vertically as possible to the fingerboard in plane A (see Fig. 8) so that the string bisects the fingertip (short nails are essential for this) (see Fig. 9).
3 Firm, though not excessive, pressure must be applied to the string

Fig. 9

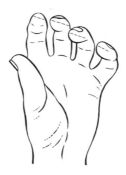

Spreading the fingers to match the spacing of the frets is a function of their secondary movement. This spread needs to be frequent adjustment to accommodate the varying fret distances as the hand moves along the fingerboard; this may seem obvious, but the extent to which fret spacings themselves vary is not always taken into consideration. For example, the distance between frets XI and XII is only *half* that between the nut and fret I;.or, to put it another way, four frets at the first position equal (by measurement) six frets at the seventh position. To the untrained hand, four consecutive frets stopped in the first position will seem almost impossible without distortion of its attitude. (This is only one of several reasons why in the early stages of learning the guitar, the lower fingerboard positions should be avoided if lasting damage to technique is not to be done.) Training the fingers to spread to the maximum required, and teaching them to adjust their spacing automatically, can only be achieved by the regular and ample practising of single-string exercises and scales in all fingerboard positions.

Fingers are only parallel to each other when closed together, and radiate fanwise when separated. When spread therefore, the second and third fingers will stand (approximately) perpendicular to the fingerboard in plane B (see Fig. 11a), but the first and fourth will lean outwards, depressing the string slightly on their sides. This does not matter very much, provided that the tip joints are kept perpendicular in plane A (see Fig. 8).

The amount of pressure needed to stop a string cleanly is impossible to specify as there are so many variables, but, as a general principle, apply the minimum strength which will give a clear note. Precision and strength are closely linked in this context, being in inverse ratio to each other; that is to say, the less accurate the placing of the fingertip, the more pressure is needed to produce a clean note. Economy of effort—as well as common sense—demands the cultivation of 'machine-like' precision in preference to the use of 'brute force'.

For the purpose of illustrating various functions of the left hand and arm in *single-note* playing, the hand may be placed with the four fingers at frets V, VI, VII, and VIII on the third string. This is possibly the most comfortable position for the hand and arm 'at rest' on the fingerboard (see Example 14).

Ex. 14

Ex. 15

Ex. 16

As with the right hand, string-crossing needs the arm to move from a stable pivot, which for the left hand is provided by the ball of the (straight) thumb in contact with the lower half of the guitar neck. When the fingers are moved to the first string (see Example 15), the elbow moves backwards (from the shoulder joint) and the wrist flattens (see Fig. 10a): the thumb rolls on the guitar neck, but without losing contact and without bending. Moving the fingers to the sixth string (see Example 16), the elbow moves forward again, and the wrist becomes almost right-angled (see Fig. 10b). Intermediate

Fig. 10a   Fig. 10b

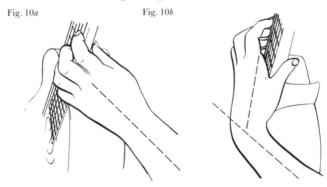

placing on strings ②, ③, ④, and ⑤ needs only a slight adjustment of the wrist to an appropriate angle between these extremes. A passage which encompasses all six strings in one position (eg a scale of A major in the fourth position) will demonstrate the smoothly graduated movement of the hand and wrist in this plane. It is vitally important that the thumb remains straight to avoid inconsistent, and therefore unreliable, placing of the fingers. The elbow, too, must travel backwards and forwards in a straight line parallel to the body, without any side-to-side deviation throughout the entire movement (see Figs. 11a and 11b); the shoulder must not be allowed to rise.

The accuracy and efficiency of this method of string-crossing rather than any other can be seen through the application of the simple mechanical principle of leverage. For example, if

Fig. 11*a*   Fig. 11*b*

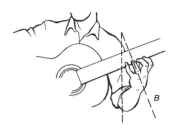
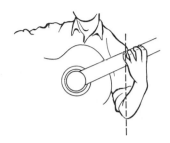

the whole forearm were to be used, pivoting from the elbow with a distance from pivot to fingertip of about 30 cm., any tiny error at the elbow would be greatly magnified, resulting in very inaccurate finger-placing. If the thumb acts as the pivot, with a distance from the fingertip of no more than about 2.5 cm., hardly any distortion can take place.

The problems which involvement of the wrist's secondary movement can cause to the right hand have been discussed in Chapter 4 (pp. 14–15). Similar difficulties can occur for the left wrist, in which secondary actions must be reduced to a minimum even if it is not possible to eliminate them altogether.

Viewed purely from the point of technical efficiency, the left forearm's ideal position is at a right angle to the fingerboard, with the elbow directly behind the hand. In the higher positions this is quite easy, but as the hand progresses downwards the attempt to maintain this right angle results in a feeling of strain in the arm as the lower positions are approached. The natural reaction to this is to leave the elbow in its original position and to use it as a pivot, swinging the forearm outwards. This has the effect of making the angle formed by the forearm and guitar neck more acute, thereby bringing the third and fourth fingers further away from the fingerboard and making all the fingers lean over towards the index (see Fig. 12). Some players, in trying to correct this inaccurate and uneconomical position, allow the wrist to bend in the secondary plane (see Fig. 13); the finger tendons, in passing

Fig. 12

Fig. 13

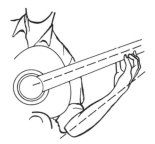

through the wrist, are then made to pull 'round a corner', which reduces both facility and strength.

Training the left hand can be a strenuous process, and indeed, some discomfort is unavoidable while joints and muscles are being coaxed into performing unaccustomed actions. Careful attention to posture and correct grip of the guitar (pp. 7–12) play an important part in minimizing this but patient and gentle persistence over a considerable period of time will be needed to make good technical habits automatic. A conscious effort must be made to hold the elbow away from the body in all positions up to the ninth if the forearm is to stay in line with the hand and collapsing of the fingers towards the thumb is to be avoided; there is also a simultaneous need to prevent the elbow from pulling backwards, which it may tend to do. Physiological principles such as this are most easily kept in mind during practising if they can be distilled into a simple maxim: for example, 'keep the elbow down and out'.

Holding the arm a little way away from the body also helps to strengthen the weak fingers (the third and fourth) by making them bear more positively on the strings, and provides an 'antidote' to the index-leaning tendency—provided the thumb is playing its part as the fulcrum for the whole arm from elbow to fingertips (see Fig. 14).

Fig. 14

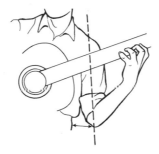

Finger action

In stopping single notes, the tip and middle joints of the fingers of the left hand must always remain bent in a relaxed curve (see p. 17)[1]—the action of lifting and replacing them on the strings being achieved by a single movement of the knuckle joint (first phalanx). Simpler actions are always more reliable, and a finger movement in which all three joints were in motion would be so complex as to make the final position of the fingertip extremely uncertain. A simple illustration explains this: a hammer-head always swings through a consistent arc when hitting a nail, provided that the operator's wrist, which is the pivot for the action, does not change its position. Supposing that the hammer were to be hinged at the junction of the head and the handle, *and* half-way along the handle; the chance of it hitting the nail accurately—or at all—would be very small. Further, if it did manage to make contact with the nail, the blow would be relatively weak, because much of the force of the impact would be absorbed by the hammer itself giving way at the hinges. The action of a finger is very similar to that of a hammer, and for maximum strength and precision, no part should be played in the stroke by the middle and tip joints.

Retaining a constant curve of the finger has two further advantages: it ensures that the tip joint is perpendicular to the fingerboard when it meets the string—most important for clean and firm stopping—and by moving only from the main joint, the backlift also is automatically reduced, giving greater economy of movement.

[1] The stopping of barrés is an exception to this.

When considering backlift, the question arises: from what distance does a finger need to approach a string? If one assumes that a' string is already in vibration from a previously struck note which must not be damped, the starting-point for the finger's action needs to be no further away than just out of range of the vibrating string's maximum amplitude. For economy of movement, therefore, no finger should ever lift more than about 0.5 cm. from the strings, and in some cases (e.g. when a string has *not* been struck previously) there is no need to lift the finger at all. Keeping the fingers down is a basic principle of left-hand technique of all stringed instruments. Lifting a finger only when there is a clear reason for doing so is a habit that should be cultivated for greatly improved legato and security. The reflex action of automatically lifting the fingers unless there is a reason for them staying down is nearly always the cause of them appearing to fly all over the fingerboard, and of much undisciplined and inaccurate left-hand work. Training the hands in economical movements means that energy is conserved; longer and more taxing works can be performed with no more expenditure of effort. Speed of execution is also increased because of the shorter distances travelled by the fingers; precision and reliability are improved as, from such a short distance as 0.5 cm., the 'target' (i.e. the string) is almost impossible to miss.

The guitar's general lack of legato and sostenuto (see pp. 71–72) is very often due to fundamental left-hand faults. The most common of these are not putting the fingers down soon enough; and lifting them, or releasing the pressure, too soon. In many passages the only way of achieving a smooth transition from one note to another is to synchronize exactly the lifting of one finger with the putting down of the other, though it frequently happens that notes can be prepared by putting down two or more fingers simultaneously. Preparation of this kind can play a large part in ensuring legato playing, which otherwise, and in other situations, is dependent on the split-second co-ordination of two left-hand finger movements with the attack of a right-hand finger.

Such instantaneous timing demands a rapid and positive action by the fingers, both in descending on to the string and in lifting off it. These two opposite movements are carried out by muscles of disproportionate strength and agility. The 'gripping' muscle (flexor) which propels the finger in towards the hand is far stronger, naturally, than the 'lifting' muscle (extensor), which, having no need of much strength in normal (non guitar-playing) activities, is relatively undeveloped. Nevertheless, lifting the finger needs to be accomplished just as quickly and accurately as putting it down. Exercises of the descending chromatic type are invaluable in developing this rapid, positive action.

A useful method of achieving perfect synchronization is to concentrate the attention on the finger which is to stay down. In Example 17, a chromatic sequence by Tarrega, as the fourth finger lefts, the third finger simultaneously presses a little harder; the second does the same when the third is lifted, and the first when the second is lifted. The effect of this is to exercise the extensor muscle of each finger independently. It should be remembered that the third and fourth fingers are weaker, and therefore more sluggish in their action, than the first and second fingers; they will obviously require far more work to bring them up to the same standard of agility. This was undoubtedly in Tarrega's mind when he devised this exercise. The pattern is one of ingenious simplicity, but little benefit will be derived from it unless one basic rule is observed: all of the fingers must be kept down on the string behind the finger which is stopping the note to be played. Put simply, this means that, when the fourth finger is stopping the note, fingers 1, 2, and 3 must also be down; when the third is stopping, 1 and 2 must be down; and when the second is stopping, 1 must be down. The first finger in fact never leaves the string throughout the exercise. Particular care must be taken over the last two notes in bars 3 and 4, as the third and fourth fingers *must* go down together.

Finger independence and split-second co-ordination are also served by the careful and repeated practising of this exercise at a very slow, metronomically even, speed.

Ex. 17. Tarrega *Exercise*

Position-changing

One of the more noticeable features of much guitar-playing in the past has been the frequent and musically inexplicable 'hiccups' in rhythm and continuity of sound. The cause of these, more often than not, is faulty left-hand technique when changing position. This has sometimes been excused as being due to the 'natural limitations' of the guitar. This is emphatically not the case; other stringed instruments face identical problems but overcame them long ago. The blame for slipshod playing which wreaks havoc on the music must lie squarely on the player and not the instrument. The admittedly difficult technique of shifting the left hand from one fingerboard position to a possibly remote one without a break in either rhythm or sound can be mastered only by adopting a systematic approach.

The arbiter of what is or what is not musically acceptable must always be the ear; however carefully a problem is analysed and worked at technically, the result will only satisfy the listener if the player's ear is supercritical, both in preparation and in presentation. This applies particularly to changes of left-hand position, at which point the music is so apt to 'come apart at the seams'.

A familiar guitaristic device for enabling the left hand to move around with relative freedom is to finger a passage in such a way as to allow an open string to be played while the hand is shifting. This is a legitimate device, but it has only limited application, and depends firstly on the passage containing an open-string note at a convenient place, and secondly on whether the sudden interpolation of the open-string sound clashes or blends with the rest of the passage. The way to decide this point (which will vary from case to case) is to try the passage first, using a stopped note for comparison. However satisfactory the open-string method of bridging the gap may seem to be, its use is really only a form of 'technical escapism', as the real problem still needs to be tackled when the notes on either side of the position change must be stopped.

A straightforward example such as occurs in a major scale can be examined to reveal a sound and reliable method (see Example 18). The essential action is a combination of arm

Ex. 18

movements: the upper arm and the forearm, in that order of importance. That is to say, the principal movement is from the shoulder, and only when the upper arm has reached its reasonable limit of travel does the forearm take over, moving from the elbow until it too cannot comfortably move any further. Hand and wrist movement are rarely needed and should only be engaged as a last resort—generally when shifting to an extreme fingerboard position.

The basic rules are firstly that the hand must move as a compact unit; up to the ninth position, the thumb remains in the same place relative to the fingers (allowing for the slight adjustment referred to on pp. 44–45) throughout, however long or short the distance travelled by the hand; a common error is to leave the thumb behind when shifting only one or two frets. (There is a different situation when extensions of the hand are employed, i.e., the four fingers stretching five or more frets. The thumb then remains stationary while either the third and fourth fingers stretch forwards to a higher fret, or the first and second stretch backwards to a lower fret. Which of these is the more convenient and economical manœuvre depends on the context.)

Secondly, the fingers must retain their general spacing; a 'crabwise' movement when ascending is almost always caused by the index finger reaching for the new position while the thumb and the rest of the hand are left behind. Conversely, when descending, allowing the thumb to move first will make the fingers collapse in the direction of the index, and bring the third and fourth fingers away from the fingerboard. Either of these faults involves unnecessary adjustment of finger-spacing by way of secondary movement of the main joints—fingers being closed together, then reopened on arrival at the new position.

A third important rule (which is often mistakenly believed to have universal application) is that the hand must remain parallel to the fingerboard before, during, and after the shift.

This rule certainly applies to all single-string position changes, and to some, but by no means all, chord sequences (see the section on chords, pp. 58–59). Where possible, there should be a guide finger which remains in contact with the string throughout the change—the index finger, for example.

The next problem concerns the amount of pressure to be applied, and for how long. If the guide finger presses uniformly the whole time, an undesirable glissando is produced and, further, friction will slow down the movement of the hand; if it releases the string completely while it is in motion, a gap in the sound will result. The right amount of pressure to apply during the shift can be gauged by touching the string with just sufficient weight to damp its open resonance, but not enough to allow a stopped note to sound. The pressure sequence in a position change is thus: (1) full pressure; (2) 'relaxed' pressure during movement; (3) full pressure again. This adjustment of pressures takes much practising to perfect, the aim being a 'silent' but entirely legato transition.

Hesitation or hurrying during position-changing can only be brought under control if the player's ear is engaged with full concentration *and* with a sense of anticipation. Unlike most other arts, the passage of time is of critical importance in music, and it is therefore a sound plan to train the mind to run a little ahead of the fingers, so that the player is always in a state of readiness. (This is also an indispensable principle for fluent sight-reading.) During the position change illustrated in Example 19*a*, the ear and brain should focus on the third note (C) while the first note (A) is being struck, and on the sixth note (B) when the fourth note (D) is played. Care must be taken to see that this 'mental' anticipation does not encourage the hand to move into position too early.

Legato performance of a position shift is greatly improved if the ear is made to pay particular attention to the full time value being given to the last note before the shift (a general principle for *all* position changes, whether of single notes or chords); a tendency to anticipate the move can easily lead to this note being cut short in favour of arriving at the new position on time.

A useful device for establishing musical standards is the 'comparative method', whereby playing the same passage in

Ex. 19*b*

two different ways can reveal any inherent weaknesses in a particular fingering. In the case of position-changing, playing the same notes in only one position but with different fingering will expose defects in legato, rhythm, glissando, etc. (see Examples 19*a*, 19*b*).

When performing, guitarists always appear to be preoccupied with their left hands, from which their eyes seldom stray. This is a strange habit for a musician: pianists are trained from an early stage of learning not to look at their hands, and who has ever seen a violinist or a cellist watching his left hand? How could a flautist, oboist, or indeed any player of an orchestral instrument, look at his hands at the same time as reading the music and watching the conductor? Is the technique of the guitar so different from all other instruments? It is not, of course, but basic technical training has tended in the past to be so ill-informed, improvised, or just plain slipshod that the student has never had pointed out to him the disadvantages of always watching his left hand; neither has he ever been shown how to play without doing so.

I once heard the great Russian cellist Rostropovich play an entire unaccompanied suite by Bach in pitch darkness in a country house. The power failed and the lights went out when he was about half-way through the Prelude, but he did not hesitate for a fraction of a second. By the time a candelabra had been fetched, the soloist had reached the last few bars of the Gigue—the last movement. He obviously had no need to see his hands at all. Neither did the jazz pianist George Shearing, who was in fact totally blind! Such technical certainty, which does not depend on vision, is by no means unusual and should be standard practice for all musicians—including guitarists. Muscular control is far more reliable than sight, and, after an initial training period, ought to provide all the guidance needed by hand and fingers. The eyes, which in any case are capable of guiding only relatively slow hand movements, can actually cause mistakes and hesitations in playing which is over-dependent on them. When their role is reduced, or even eliminated altogether, acute aural awareness begins to develop automatically.

All hand and finger movements will need visual guidance during the 'training period' just mentioned, but it is very important that the eyes should not be allowed just to stare aimlessly at the hand or the fingerboard. A shift from (say) third to seventh position as in Example 18 is accomplished by focusing on the point just behind the eighth fret as early as possible—preferably while the first note (C) is being sounded. Directing the eyes at a new point means that they see a blurred image for a moment while they refocus, which causes the finger to be aimed at a spot which is not itself clearly defined; the hand movement therefore lacks certainty, precision, and speed. Anticipatory movement of the eyes allows them to focus clearly on the 'target' fret before the hand moves. A simple analogy with the firing of a 'missile' (the hand) at a target (the new position) will illustrate the importance of using vision constructively in training. If a missile (say an arrow) is to be fired at a target, it would be quite futile to try and guide it by watching it in flight; the eyes must first focus on the target before the arrow is released.

After much practising of 'visually guided' position-changing, in a great variety of patterns and distances, the foundations will have been laid for 'blind' shifting. The temptation to look must now be firmly resisted—even when mistakes occur—the ear and muscular control providing the only guidance. Confidence will quickly develop when it is found how accurate and reliable this method can be; many new applications of it will be discovered which are by no means confined to use of the index as a guide finger, or even to the need to keep a finger in contact with a string at all.

Chords

The action of stopping single notes requires the left-hand fingers to move only from their main joints, with middle and tip joints held in a relaxed curve during this movement. However, when two or more strings are to be stopped simultan-

Ex. 20

eously, departure from this principle and some adjustment of these joints become necessary (see Example 20). To reach the sixth string in this unlikely, though possible, example, the second finger has to straighten (especially at the middle joint), though even this may not be enough to allow a lateral (across the fingerboard) separation of the fingertips, which, having previously been in one line, now need placing about 4.5 cm. apart. The first finger is therefore also called upon to help by increasing its bend at tip and middle joints. If at all possible, strings must always be stopped by the exact tip of the finger (see p. 44), so this sharing of the adjustment between the two fingers helps to ensure that neither is excessively distorted. Stability of the hand as a whole, and minimal deviation of fingers from the relaxed-curve position, are extremely important rules; shared adjustment allows each finger to stay closer to the ideal bend. This adjustment becomes more difficult when their positions are reversed (see Example 21), as their unequal lengths adversely affect the stretch across the fingerboard.

Ex. 21

Whatever the left-hand pattern, hand, wrist, and arm must first be positioned so that the fingers themselves have only to make small final adjustments. In much chord-playing, most of these adjustments can be made 'in mid-air', while the arm is positioning itself or while it is in motion during a change of fingerboard position. A guide finger or fingers will help to stabilize the hand as well as making the change more legato.

The 'rule' which has been accepted for many years that the hand must be kept parallel to the edge of the fingerboard at all times is fallacious and physiologically impossible, as a single chord is sufficient to demonstrate (see Example 22). To meet the basic criteria of fingers standing on their tips and being kept right up to the frets, the elbow must be held well away from the side when playing this chord, unless there is to be some very undesirable distortion of the wrist. The back of the hand is thus brought to an angle of at least forty-five degrees to the fingerboard's edge. The opposite extreme position for the arm is shown by a chord of D major, played in the second position (see Example 23); the fourth finger, though the short-

Ex. 22   Ex. 23

est, must now reach further across the fingerboard than any of the others. To make this possible, the hand has to be angled slightly beyond the parallel position, with the elbow held in to the side. This illustrates the first plane of movement of the left arm; to allow full flexibility, the whole arm must be free to move from the shoulder, pivoting on the ball of the thumb, making variable alignment through an arc of ninety degrees possible. The positioning of the elbow at the extremes of this arc, or at any point between them, is governed by the usual criterion—fingers up to the frets. By using pure arm movement (avoiding wrist distortion) for the 'coarse positioning' of the hand, the majority of chords will fall readily under the fingers, which will then need minimum adjustment. Figures 15a–e, which show the different positions of the arm for Example 24, illustrate this point clearly.

Ex. 24

Adjustment of the arm-to-fingerboard angles in the second plane is also essential to the accurate and economical stopping of any chord; the all-important point of contact between the thumb and the guitar neck is the pivot for both movements.

Fig. 15*a*

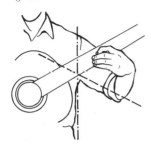

Fig. 15*b*

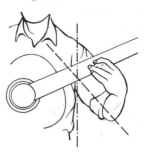

Fig. 15*c*

Fig. 15*d*

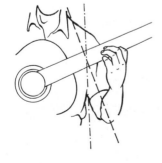

Fig. 15*e*

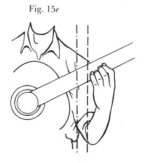

This second plane is the forward/backward movement of the forearm which has already been described in the section on string-crossing for single-note playing (p. 46). The same method is used in playing chords. Example 25 illustrates the extremes of wrist position for two contrasting chords. The thumb, the essential pivotal base, needs to form part of a compact grouping with the fingers whether the chord spans two, three, or four frets. The most stable and efficient support for all the fingers is provided if the thumb is placed as nearly as possible to the centre of their grouping. Care is needed during changes of position to see that the thumb does not get 'left behind', having to catch up only when the fingers have arrived at the new position. Alignment of hand to fingerboard never does quite catch up if this is allowed to happen!

Ex. 25

Placing fingers in the order in which the notes are to be played is a familiar technique in arpeggiated textures; it can also be used in pure chordal patterns and sequences, if only as a 'slow practising device' for training the fingers in very accurate placing. It is also a useful method of building a chord from a secure foundation.

To sum up the procedure for positioning the left hand and fingers in chord-playing: first the hand and thumb are positioned by arm movement in two planes (forwards/backwards and side to side), then the final finger adjustments are made. The two arm movements may be combined for maximum economy, though rehearsing them separately to begin with will establish a clearer understanding of their different functions. In most cases, realignment of the fingers can also take place simultaneously with the arm adjustments and any change of fingerboard position. When properly co-ordinated, this method can ensure practically instantaneous chord changes.

Left-hand extensions (stretches)

Any chord which spans more than four frets may be described as involving a 'stretch', though it must be remembered that due to diminishing fret-spacing, six frets at the seventh position (for example) requires no greater spread of the fingers than four frets at the first position. Physiologically, the constraint on the hand is not simply one of finger length, but also the limited scope for extension in this (secondary) plane of the main joints of the fingers. The 'webs' between the fingers, too, restrict the spread, but with gentle exercising over a period of time, these can gradually be stretched to increase the overall span of the hand. Impatient or too violent attempts to improve the spread can cause injury; the fingers must be allowed to make the effort entirely with their own muscles, without help from the right hand, and certainly without artificial aids such as a golf ball!

It is to be expected that where a chord includes a stretch, there will be occasions when the fingers are unable to stand on their tips, and sometimes cannot even reach right up to the frets. In this case, the only possible compensation for lack of precision is increased finger pressure to ensure clean stopping.

As with most technical problems, a few minutes spent in studying and thinking about the nature of the difficulty can save many hours of painful and often unrewarding work. Context is important to the method of approaching extensions of the left-hand fingers; stretches may be forward, backward, or overall 'finger-spreading', according to the chord shape. It is generally true to say that the extended position of the hand does not have the same stability as when the fingers are spaced normally, so the positioning of the thumb becomes doubly important. Though it may not necessarily be placed in the geometrical centre of the hand, it must feel as though it is counterbalancing the pressure of all the fingers equally— except when a barré forms part of the chord, when the thumb must be placed directly opposite the index finger as usual.

Certain extensions are only needed momentarily, the fingers then returning immediately to the closed position; in these cases, the most reliable method is to allow the thumb to remain in the same place on the guitar neck throughout the passage.

Another type of 'extension' is encountered when the left hand is stopping notes above the twelfth fret: for maximum security, the thumb is placed in the corner where the neck of the guitar joins its body, the wrist is brought well forward, and the fingers reach over the guitar body to the remaining frets (XIII to XIX). The relatively close and diminishing fret-spacing means that this is not really a stretch, but simply a different alignment of the hand to allow for the comparative inaccessibiity of this part of the fingerboard. While moving to these higher positions from the main part of the fingerboard does not usually cause any problem, returning can be awkward. The solution to this particular problem is to allow the thumb to retain its position, letting the fingers 'pass' it until it has regained its normal place in relation to them, when the hand continues downwards as a unit.

The barré and half-barré

Holding several strings down on to the fingerboard with the index finger is probably the most strenuous activity that the left hand has to perform, particularly if the barré has to be held continuously for any length of time. Sheer strength is no guarantee of clean stopping, though clearly extra exertion and endurance are called for.

In normal (non guitar-playing) activities, the most powerful grip can be achieved by the thumb and index finger if their tips are directly opposed to each other; to adopt this attitude, they need to be curved by bending at the joints. As the fingerboard is flat and the strings lie in a straight line across it, a bent index finger cannot possibly stop them all evenly, however much strength is applied. A perfectly straight implement such as a pencil would be ideal for the purpose; but the finger is not straight, having indentations at the joints with fleshy bumps in between them. It can be made to simulate the pencil only if it is stretched out to its fullest extent from knuckle to tip—as if pointing at a distant object!

The straight finger has not always been deemed to be a physical necessity for playing barrés; one or two nineteenth-century guitar-makers built instruments with slightly curved fingerboards (similar to a violin or cello) to accommodate the curve of a relaxed index finger. This experiment was quickly abandoned, as it became apparent that the guitarist must adapt himself to his instrument rather than the reverse. Though a straight finger provides a slightly less powerful grip than a bent one, the muscle at the base of thumb is capable of being trained to a very high degree of strength, and can be made to compensate for the attitude which the finger is compelled to adopt for the clean stopping of barrés.

The correct positioning of the thumb is even more vital for the barré than for any other kind of stopping; it needs to be placed lower on the guitar neck, and to be perfectly straight at both joints. Pushing the wrist well forward helps to keep the index finger straight and parallel to its fret, and counteracts a tendency to apply the grip by pulling with the arm (see Figure 16).

Fig. 16

When a barré forms part of a chord pattern, the thumb should move to a position directly opposite the index finger, regardless of the placing of any other fingers; moving it away from its normal position in the centre of the fingers' span enables it to give more support where it is needed most. The balanced grip and straight finger are emphasized still further if an attempt is made to gain a sensation of squeezing harder with the middle of the finger (i.e. on the third and fourth strings in a full barré).

Viewed from every angle, the index finger should be straight. There is a common tendency to allow the hand to lean over towards the nut of the guitar; this makes the index finger lie on its side, thereby drawing the other fingers over towards it, bunching them up and displacing them. Such a position is inclined to make the index finger rely on help from the others, so making it less likely that it will develop its own strength: it is, in reality, a method of bringing pressure to bear on the fingerboard by using a 'twisting' action of the wrist instead of a grip between thumb and finger. Keeping the elbow well away from the side, and the wrist forwards, will ensure that the strings are held down only by the face of the index finger, and that the other fingers are perpendicular and not leaning. In particular, the second finger must not touch the index finger, and certainly must not be allowed to rest on top of it!

Some barré chords are difficult to stop cleanly due to the index finger's tendency to lie at an angle to the fret instead of parallel to it. Example 26 shows the muffling of the top string

Ex. 26

and then the bottom string. In both cases, the slight misalignment of the hand, and therefore the barré, are caused by the necessary placing of the other fingers. Much care and perseverance are needed to coax them into accurate placing without disturbing the barré, for which a straight and parallel position must always take precedence over all other finger adjustments.

The loosely termed 'half'-barré (meaning any number of strings from two to five) necessitates a modification of the full-barré hand position in order to accommodate the index finger's 'surplus' length. Withdrawing the wrist to allow only the tip, or tip and middle, joints of the index finger to press the strings is a faulty, though often used method. It is wrong for two reasons: it encourages the use of 'arm-pull' to obtain pressure, and it tends to allow the finger to bend up at the tip joint, resulting in unclear stopping of the top string.

A far more secure and reliable half-barré is obtained if, by pushing the wrist forwards, the index finger is made to bend inwards at the tip joint, with the middle knuckle pointing upwards at an acute angle (see Figure 17). This gives a very strong grip between thumb and finger, while maintaining the forward position of the wrist that is needed for other notes in the chord to be accessible to the remaining fingers. The thumb must be kept straight, and low on the guitar neck, as for the full barré.

Fig. 17

Slurs

The 'slur' in guitar music has often been regarded in the past merely as a convenient technical device whose effect on musical phrasing etc. was coincidental and of secondary importance. A more musically enlightened view is beginning to permeate the world of the guitar, and with it more sparing and selective use of this valuable piece of technique.

The most obvious effect of slurring is to achieve a smoother, or more legato, transition from note to note than even the most perfect right-hand attack can give—however well this is co-ordinated with a well-developed left-hand technique. Ascending and descending slurs use entirely different technical methods, but in either case, only the first note of a slurred pair is struck by the right hand. As the subsequent note(s) are sounded by the action of a left-hand finger alone, difficulties of exact synchronization of the hands are considerably reduced—which may explain the overuse of slurs in earlier times as a means of demonstrating superficial virtuosity!

The ascending slur needs only a sharp, hammer-like striking of the string by the left-hand fingertip. The action of the finger is identical to that normally used in stopping, but with a firmer impact. It is of especial importance that the tip joint of the finger is perpendicular, and that the tip itself is exactly bisected by the string, to obtain a clear, firm tone: accuracy matters more than strength.

The finger action for the descending slur differs fundamentally from all other left-hand techniques: propulsion of the tip is by movement of the middle joint, with no part in the action being played by the main joint. Beginning with both fingers on the string, the upper note is first sounded by the right hand, then the left-hand fingertip is withdrawn sharply towards the palm of the hand. At the same time, light pressure downwards on to the fingerboard causes the finger to 'snap' off the string, thus sounding the lower note. This action must come from the finger alone, without any movement of the arm—either sideways or backwards.

Possible faults which can arise from this brisk pulling of the string across the fingerboard include pulling it out of tune, and in the case of the top string, pulling it off the edge of the fingerboard altogether. If the string is pulled out of alignment in this way, the slurred note will lack crispness and precise rhythmic control. This tendency is countered by simply pushing in the opposite direction (i.e. towards the bass strings) with the finger which remains on the string, stopping the lower note. This push–pull action should keep the string stationary in its original line, giving a crisper sound and better intonation.

In order to develop a positive, controlled descending-slur technique, it helps to practise on an inner string with a kind of apoyando, bringing the slurring finger down on to the fingerboard, and coming to rest against the next (higher) string. Stability of hand and arm must be maintained at all times.

While the exclusive use of ascending or descending slurs limits the sequence to a compass of four chromatic notes after the initial right-hand attack, combining the two techniques means that fairly long passages can be played slurred (see Example 27). Older editions of guitar music sometimes indicate that a note is to be played with a slur on a string which has not been struck previously with the right hand (see Example 28); this is not a very successful technique, as the resulting sound is usually too weak to be effective.

A problem often arises when descending slurs are needed while a barré is being held, especially if the second finger has

Ex. 27   Ex. 28

to execute the slur on the top string. The acute bend needed by this finger can easily cause the barré to be displaced, but this should never be allowed to happen; very slow, careful practising will improve the finger's flexibility and independence.

As slurred passages are easier to play at a fast speed, guitarists are often tempted to use them more than is justified by musical sense. Apart from the sometimes bizarre effect on phrasing, this can easily cause jerky playing. It is worth remembering that rhythmically even playing gives a better impression of speed than faster, but poorly controlled, execution.

6

CO-ORDINATION

THE piano has occasionally been described as a 'tuned percussion' instrument. This implied limitation is one that it shares with the guitar—the lack of a genuine sostenuto such as bowed strings, woodwind, brass, or the human voice enjoy, means that after its initial attack, every note decays rapidly, making long-held notes impossible. In the case of the guitar, the problem is compounded by (1) shorter string-lengths (which, for all but a few notes, are a compromise); and (2) the vital importance of the exact synchronization of the fingers of the two hands. This last factor can be a severely inhibiting factor to legato, which in any case is one of the guitar's main weaknesses.

When the right-hand attack fails to coincide exactly with firm stopping of the string by the left-hand finger, the first casualty is legato; the guitar allows no tolerance, or leeway, of even a fraction of a second in the production of an acceptable basic sound. Such precise timing is essential for even the simplest transition from one note to the next, but it is no less vital when technical complexities such as position-changing, difficult chord patterns, stretches, etc. are involved. Co-ordination is often the first area in which faults begin to appear when practising has been neglected for some time, and the last thing to return when it is resumed.

The techniques of both hands have already been examined in some detail; if basic faults remain in either, co-ordinating them will be much more difficult, if not impossible. In the past, the standard recipe for good co-ordination has been to position the left-hand finger a fraction of a second before striking with the right hand. Apart from the obvious difficulty of attempting to judge this 'microsecond' with consistent accuracy, the whole mental attitude of caution which this 'principle' encourages causes hesitancy to be built in to the technique. A much more positive approach is needed for the realization of the guitar's maximum legato capability.

The right hand should always be thought of as the one which sets and maintains the pace, and which regulates the left hand; the latter must learn to 'keep up'. The tendency of allowing the right hand to wait for the left to position itself, especially in complex chord sequences, is one of the causes of 'technical rubato', i.e. hesitations and changes of tempo which are devoid of musical sense, so common in much guitar-playing. The aim should be for the left-hand finger to reach its maximum pressure on the string at exactly the same moment as the right-hand finger contacts the string. Many variable factors, some physiological and some purely technical, tend to prevent this from happening: the differing finger-strengths (and therefore speed of reaction) of both hands, and whether the passage is ascending or descending, are but two examples of the type of obstacle to perfect co-ordination which has to be overcome. If the left hand is incapable of stopping the notes in exact synchronization with a metronomically controlled right-hand attack, then the practising speed must be reduced, and reduced again, until a supercritical ear—the final arbiter—is entirely satisfied with the result.

7

TECHNIQUES OF
INTERPRETATION

'MUSIC', said a distinguished pianist in the course of a lecture a few years ago, 'is a song and dance act!' An over-simple definition perhaps, particularly as dramatic or toccata-type music, written mainly for the purpose of displaying the performer's technical skill, is omitted from it. Nevertheless, most 'composed' music owes its origins to either singing or dancing, however remote the connection, and this is the point that the lecturer was making.

To take first the 'singing' quality: players of all instruments strive for a cantabile tone in imitation of the human voice. Beautiful sound has an immediate impact on the listener; he quickly loses interest in a performance from which it is absent, for no other quality can entirely redeem such a performance. Cultivation of beautiful tone must therefore be considered a priority. Imagine a vocal quality in every part; better still, try singing each line before playing it. Nadia Boulanger, the re-nowned teacher, said: 'Nothing can replace the voice—the voice is the most important—a man must sing!' (She might have added that you do not need a trained voice, or for that matter much of a voice at all!)

The guitar, like the piano, is a 'tuned percussion' instru-ment, and therefore lacks genuine legato and sostenuto—especially the latter. The guitarist must work very hard to develop both the aural awareness and finger co-ordination which alone will enable him to produce a flowing line in simulation of the voice.

Phrasing and articulation

Beautiful tone, however important, will not of itself guarantee a musical performance. An unphrased passage in music makes no more sense to the listener than a passage of prose read without punctuation or modulation of the voice; try reading this page aloud, in a monotone, without pausing for breath, and ignoring all full stops and commas! Singers, wind-instrument players, and bowed-string players are all compelled by the technical demands of their instruments (breathing or bowing) to pay very careful attention to phrase lengths. They do not, of course, just break the line wherever it is technically convenient to do so, but plan the overall phrasing in advance according to musical sense, and then adapt their technical practising to fit this.

The guitar does not have the same kind of technically compelling need for phrasing as other instruments, with the result that guitarists are hardly aware of its existence. In printed guitar music, too, phrase markings are rare. It is theoretically possible to perform an unbroken line of indefinite length on the guitar, and many guitarists, to whom the cultivation of cantabile (thinking 'horizontally') does not come naturally, tend to allow the instrument's left-hand technique to dictate arbitrary mid-phrase breaks, blurring of phrase-endings, and unmusical hesitations and 'hiccups'.

Complex finger-pattern movements, in which the stopping of notes in one voice can interrupt, or in other ways influence, the fingering of those in another voice; the generally 'vertical' configuration of chord shapes; restrictions imposed by the barré; less than perfect position-changing ('technical staccato')—all of these technical problems, and many others, contribute to the guitar's seemingly in-built 'unmusicality'. Technical barriers to musical phrasing, which can only be overcome by the conscious cultivation of a feeling for 'line' (melody), and the natural 'breathing points' in the music, can, paradoxically, also be used to advantage if they are made to coincide with these points.

A sensitive awareness of 'line', best developed by singing (actual or in the mind), ultimately gives the player the confidence to write the phrasing on the music (as a violinist would write bowings) and then to translate these into technical instructions in the form of fingering, string and position-markings, etc. Example 29 is a transposed fragment of a tune for oboe from Tchaikovsky's fourth Symphony, and illustrates

the method of fingering that is needed to adhere to the composer's phrasing. (No slurs; all notes struck by the right hand.)

Equal in importance with good phrasing is articulation.
Simply defined, phrasing might be described as the joining-
together of notes to form musical 'sentences' (phrases), and

Ex. 29. Tchaikovsky *Fourth Symphony*

articulation as a slight detaching of notes, either to separate
notes or phrases from each other or to give certain notes a
particular attack or rhythmic 'bite'. Example 29 shows how
both legato phrasing and detached articulation form an integral part of the interpretation of a song-like passage, though
each exists only by contrast with the other.

Legato phrasing of a single line needs greater care on the
guitar than on most other instruments, for the guitar enjoys—
or suffers from—a type of sonority in which the harmonic
aspect plays an important part. This is the often evocative, if
somewhat peculiar, effect known as 'overholding'. Overlapping resonances can give an extraordinary richness to
broken-chord textures, but they can also make complete non-
sense of the composer's melodies and harmonies if allowed to
occur haphazardly (compare Examples 31 and 37). Notes
which ring on beyond their written time values can cause
diffused sound, unintentional dissonances, and unclear articulation. This is especially true when open strings are used
with the degree of unplanned freedom which has been customary in the past, though it also occurs when the fingers
holding stopped notes are left down for too long—mostly for
technical reasons. 'Technical staccato' has a companion in
'technical sostenuto'! Examples 30*a–c*, a simple minor scale
fingered in two different ways, illustrates this point. In

Ex. 30*a*   Ex. 30*b*   Ex. 30*c*

Example 30a, three open-string notes will continue sounding (owing to the impossibility of damping them) and creating the dissonances shown in Example 30b, whereas in Example 30c no two notes can sound simultaneously except at the points marked *, where care must be taken to release the first finger at precisely the same moment as the fourth stops the G. Indiscriminate use of open strings causes the further problem of tonal unevenness; they usually have a more strident quality, and tend therefore to stand out from the rest of the texture.

A composer will occasionally specify a crisp, non-sustained resonance, even where the writing appears to have a harmonic content; Example 31, from Lennox Berkeley's Theme and

Ex. 31. Berkeley *Theme and Variations for Guitar*

mf non legato   *Reproduced by kind permission of Fentone Music Publishers Ltd.*

Variations for Guitar, must be fingered in such a way as to cause each note to be damped by the stopping of its successor if the composer's non legato direction is to be followed.

Conversely, a passage with a very similar-looking texture may, by implication, need the full harmony of the broken chords to sound. Here, too, very carefully designed fingering is essential so that some notes are held beyond their written duration, while others are damped immediately. Two bars

Ex. 32a. Bach *Prelude*

Ex. 32b Bach *Prelude*

from a well-known Bach Prelude show clearly the harmonic pattern (see Examples 32*a* and *b*; I have added two bass notes (bracketed) in the block-chord illustration (Example 32*b*) so as to make clear the implied bass line). As is usual in Bach's music, there is, in addition to the harmonic element, a 'horizontal' or contrapuntal interest; it is not always in the top voice, but it too requires some notes to be sustained for continuity. To be sure that all such resonances are intentional, a preliminary analysis of the piece's structure is needed; this gives an insight into the harmonic implications which, in turn, form the basis for planning the fingering.

Articulation has a special significance in music whose origins lie in dance-forms, for it is vital to rhythmic expression. Examples 33*a* and *b* (illustrated onomatopoeically) show how separating the quavers and semi-quavers in the middle of the

Ex. 33*a* Scarlatti *Sonata*   Ex. 33*b*

tra - la-la-la - la - tra - la   rum - ti-ti-tum-tum - tra - la

bar in Example 33*b* give a 'lift' and 'bounce' to the rhythm which is lacking in Example 33*a*. Technical methods of achieving this momentary damping of the strings have been fully explored in Chapter 4. Either hand may be used depending on the context, but in this example the right hand will be found to be more effective (rapid replacement of fingers on the strings which have just been struck), especially as the bass-pedal note F sharp must be allowed to sound for its full value. Care must be taken at all times to avoid the involuntary, or 'technically convenient', staccato which can be caused by faulty left-hand movement or defective right-hand attack.

Tempo and rhythm

The problem of choosing the 'right' tempo for a piece of music affects the guitarist no less than other musicians, but with more likelihood of a decision being made for technical rather than musical reasons.

Tempo indications on the music (eg 'andante', 'moderato', 'allegro', etc.) are no more than approximations, telling the player that the chosen speed should be within certain limits. The precise tempo depends on his overall view of how the piece is to be interpreted, and even those relatively rare guitar works which include the composer's metronome mark can, nevertheless, sound equally convincing, or even more effective, at a quite different tempo—the general consensus amongst musicians is that composers tend to indicate speeds which are a little too fast! Composers, on the other hand, sometimes find executants unconvincing in their choice of tempos. According to Wagner, 'The majority of performances of instrumental music are faulty; conductors fail to find the true tempo because they are ignorant of singing. I have not yet met a Musikdirektor who, be it with good or bad voice, can really sing a melody!'

A piece which in one performance sounds just right, can in another player's hands seem too slow or too fast even when taken at exactly the same speed. An impression of lethargy or haste is almost always due to a failure to direct the fingers according to a clear, predetermined musical plan. One useful tip is to 'count yourself in'—to count silently, say, two bars at the chosen tempo before beginning to play. This avoids the common tendency of starting in a headlong rush and then having to slow down—or break down—after a few bars. It is not at all easy to make a musically convincing adjustment to the tempo in mid-performance, so it is better not to have to try, by being certain that the speed is as intended from the first notes.

If the guitarist's Achilles' heel is rhythm (and there is little doubt in the minds of most musicians that it is!), there is a strong possibility that the cause has something to do with the instrument's virtual isolation from corporate music-making, and the absence of any formal training in rhythmic disciplines which is a natural consequence of this deficiency.

A truly musical performance can never be completely metronomical; some elasticity in tempo is essential to allow the music to breathe and to 'come alive'. Rubato can take the form of quite substantial or almost imperceptible departures from a strict metre, and has been described as 'bending, but not breaking time'. The number of possible nuances is infinite, but in the very broadest terms it could be said that climaxes of phrases often seem to call for slightly more emphasis and 'holding back' in the rhythm; i.e. stressing a note and holding it for longer than its written value, and that this sometimes requires preparation in the shape of a small rallentando in the approach to the climactic note. Ends of phrases, too, usually, thought not invariably, suggest a slackening of the tempo, just as in speech the pitch of the voice tends to fall towards the end of a sentence. The opposite of these rallentandos and ritenutos is the accelerando, which is often associated with an increase in tension towards a point of (musical) excitement; this needs more careful and sparing use, and does not fit naturally into music of all periods. All fluctuations in tempo must be applied with discretion; guard against taking excessive liberties which distort the underlying pulse to the point where rhythmic momentum is lost altogether.

If, as so often happens, technical convenience rather than interpretative insight dictates the use of rubato, the result will be garbled and unmusical. It must be said that some renowned performers have attempted to disguise the technical motive behind their unstable rhythm and misplaced or exaggerated use of rubato by the sheer force of their personal conviction. The effect can never be entirely convincing to a musical listener, having something of the 'circus' element in it. Reginald Smith Brindle, composer and Professor of Music at Surrey University, asserts that 'The art of rubato is far above the menial task of helping us to overcome our shortcomings. It is what turns technique into musicianship, and what makes bare notation become mystical poetry. We are born with a feeling for it, and it cannot be taught. But the first step towards possessing it is to become aware.' A method of preventing the insidious development of 'technical rubato' is first to play the piece through in strict time, noting carefully all the places which could give rise to hesitation, slowing down, or hurrying. These must then be worked at until they no longer present technical problems. Then, putting the guitar aside, read through the music, mentally 'listening' to phrases and lines, points of tension and repose, and mark these on the score. After working in this way for some time, a genuine interpretation should begin to emerge and to take shape. This musical 'image' must then be translated into technical terms on the guitar; logical fingerings will be suggested by it, and purely technical distortions will be avoided.

Volume and dynamics

Compared to other instruments, the dynamic range of the guitar is limited to those levels of volume below *mf* on the piano; an orchestral tutti *ff* is far beyond the sound-world of the guitar. This is not necessarily the handicap that is sometimes supposed, as the instrument's softer sounds can have a unique appeal, though it does cause some problems of balance when playing in an ensemble, and especially when a guitarist is the soloist in a concerto.

Even this restricted dynamic range is seldom exploited to the full by guitarists, who can very often be heard playing at a uniform *mp* throughout a performance. Dull playing of this kind is almost always due to a failure to recognize the importance of dynamic variety as an integral part of expression, as well as to technical insecurity.

Technical assurance, in the shape of a firm, powerful right-hand attack, is the essential base from which all control of volume levels must begin. It is an error to imagine that the effort devoted to achieving greater volume is only intended to make the guitar into a louder instrument. More expressive playing than the guitarist's customary monotone allows can be achieved with a wider dynamic range. Even in the nineteenth century this fact was recognized by Fernando Sor, who longed for a guitar with greater volume 'in order to diminish it!' It is always easier to attenuate the sound from a strong and well-projected starting-point than if the attack is habitually weak and tentative; in the latter case, it is practically impossible to increase the volume, as the necessary muscular strength and certainty simply do not exist. From a 'position of strength' the whole of the guitar's dynamic range may be developed, from the merest whispered tirando pianissimo, through to the loudest apoyando notes.

Such fine control of right hand technique needs conscious training, and must not be left to chance—or the inspiration (!) of the moment. Example 34 shows how difficult it is to achieve

Ex. 34

an even grading of tone from *pp* to *mf* and back again. There should be no perceptible change in timbre as tirando is gradually superseded by apoyando around the middle of the scale.

It is self-evident, but all too often forgotten in practice, that a passage which is to be played with a crescendo must begin quietly, and, conversely, one requiring a diminuendo must begin loudly. If these simple rules are ignored, the passage will be played in the usual guitarist's monotone.

As with most technical/expressive devices, a measure of exaggeration is needed in all changes of volume if they are not to sound timid or even to go unnoticed. The listener does not hear all of the nuances which to the player may seem quite clear; much of what he *thinks* he is doing is going on already in his head. The need for overstatement applies throughout the guitar's dynamic spectrum, which, being much narrower than that of other instruments, can only show drama, excitement, repose, and all the shades of expression in between by the use of much bolder contrasts.

Tone colour and registration

In the opinion of one well-known guitarist, 'Timbre is the supreme resource of the guitar.' Guitarists are well-aware of their instrument's capacity for tonal variety, and most of them exploit it. Colour is certainly an important feature of guitar tone, few other instruments have the guitar's range and flexibility in either shading or contrast of timbre, but all too often this extra facility is used haphazardly, or as a substitute for real expression. Some years ago, *The Times* music critic, reviewing a Wigmore Hall guitar recital, wrote that the soloist's 'capricious and illogical tone colouring played havoc with the early music in the programme; this improvisatory style mattered less when it came to romantic music, but even here far more taste and finish were needed'.

It is important for the guitarist to keep tone colour in perspective and not to treat it merely as an 'effect' or novelty, thus only trivializing rather than enhancing the music. I am reminded of a tutor written in about 1910 by a guitarist who claimed to be a pupil of Tarrega's. Many pages of his book were devoted to various effects which could be obtained on the guitar, including a page of detailed instructions on 'How to imitate the cracked voice of an old woman' (sic)! Such 'party tricks' are beneath contempt, and have no place in a treatise on serious musical performance. Many such instruction books for the guitar place far too much emphasis on effects such as pizzicato, tremolo, harmonics, tambora, etc., which are described in great detail, while the essential substance of basic technique is skimmed over very superficially. Most players will have devised their own methods for achieving these effects, which for the most part require positions of the hands and use of fingers which cannot conform to orthodoxy.

Free use of registration can enhance or ruin a fine musical performance, but it cannot save one which is defective in the more fundamental qualities of sensitive phrasing and dynamic control which are the life-blood of any genuinely musical interpretation, and of which they must form an integral part. They are the basic ingredients of the 'cake', whereas variety of timbre, though a valuable expressive bonus, is merely the 'icing'. It is easy to see how contrasts and shading between tasto and ponticello are more attractive to the guitarist, as they are far easier technically than the painstaking right-hand control demanded by graded dynamics and careful phrasing. Registrational 'fireworks' offer the player the added attraction of immediate and spectacular appeal. Though most solo instruments do not have the same range of tonal variety as the guitar, they are all capable of being played with as great, or greater, depth of expression, mainly because their players pay much more attention to phrasing and dynamics than the majority of guitarists. Beethoven is said to have described the guitar as 'a miniature orchestra'. Planning the use of its tonal resources might be thought of as similar to orchestration, and needing no less careful application; it can play a significant part in highlighting the interpretation if well done.

The technical method for varying the right-hand attack between the sound-hole and the bridge is very simple: the whole arm should pivot from the shoulder without any alteration in the angles at the wrist or elbow. This movement brings the point of contact between forearm and guitar edge closer to the wrist as the hand approaches the bridge. Shifting the balancing-point in this way makes the arm less stable than when it is in its normal position, but since it does not usually remain thus for very long, the temporary slight increase in stress is of no great importance. The 'whole-arm' movement from the shoulder has an added advantage in that, as the hand approaches the bridge, the alignment of the palm becomes more parallel to the strings, and the nails therefore become more 'square on'. This emphasizes still further the sharper, brighter quality of ponticello tone. The movement itself is more economical therefore, with greater tonal contrast being obtained for less distance travelled and smaller deviation from the normal position.

8

PRACTISING

THE pianist Artur Rubinstein was stopped in a New York street one day by a lady who said: 'Excuse me, how do I get to Carnegie Hall?' He looked at her and said: 'Practise!' Practising is a matter of forming habits, and it therefore entails an almost unlimited amount of repetition. It is learning to do something which you could not do before, or doing something very much better than you could do it before; training the muscles, tendons, and joints to work in a controlled and consistent way—mechanics plus thought all the time.

Practising must begin in the mind; any practising done without the mind engaged retards progress. Putting right unthinking faults takes far longer than acquiring bad habits. (Vivian Joseph, cellist)

Do not expect to master any particular difficulty in a single day. Even with, say, thirty repetitions of a problem passage, played slowly, with full concentration, metronomic evenness, and hypercritical attention to detail, fingers cannot learn new habits at once; the same routine must be repeated day after day for at least a week before any improvement can be expected to show.

If I miss a single day's practising, it is enough to make a difference to a concert—not so much that anyone else would notice, but enough to affect my own fulfilment. (Barry Douglas, concert pianist)

The rate of progress depends as much on the quality of the work done as it does on the length of each practising-session and the number of sessions per day. As a general guide, little and often is always preferable to 'marathon' sessions, when falling concentration begins to diminish the amount of benefit being derived after about forty-five minutes.

The most important precept for all music learning must be: absorb a *little* over *long periods*. Never rush yourself; never *be* rushed; let things soak through, sink in, and eventually fall into place. A carefully planned, well-structured strategy is needed right from the start. (Philippe Monnet, *Guitar International*)

For any progress at all to be possible, a clear sense of purpose and direction is needed. Practising aimlessly, and without the attention being focused on a goal, is mere 'doodling' and time-wasting. The prevalent habit of just 'playing through' pieces leaves all the technical blemishes and musical muddle undisturbed, if not actually confirmed.

It is very dangerous to allow a single mistake in rhythm, phrasing, articulation, or technique generally to pass uncorrected; the more this happens, the more ingrained the faults will become, but what is far worse, the more numbed and anaesthetised will the self-critical faculty also become. (Peter Norris, Director of Music, The Yehudi Menuhin School)

A carefully planned schedule, written out and placed on the music-stand, will, if strictly followed, ensure that every minute is used productively and that practising does not degenerate into pointless, semi-automatic activity.

The time devoted to practising is a matter of personal choice, depending on a conjunction of the necessary, the desirable, and the possible. The shorter the available time, the more important the strategy regulating the use of that time. (Philippe Monnet)

Slow practising is the key to ultimate technical mastery; not just slower than usual, but *really* slow, and with meticulous attention to rhythm. Practising one meaningful exercise—or a difficulty extracted from a piece—very slowly, twenty times, will prove far more fruitful than playing through twenty different exercises once each.

I like music that can be played slowly! (Igor Stravinsky)

As a preliminary 'locating' exercise, position the fingers carefully on the fourth string, somewhere in the middle of the fingerboard; then, having spaced them accurately to the frets, and made sure that the tips are exactly bisected by the string (see p. 44), press firmly for about ten seconds. This will make 'grooves' in the fingertips, which will then act as guides to precision for the exercises and scales which follow.

If I had only one hour a day in which to practise, I would practise scales, and if it were two hours, it would be more scales. (Jascha Heifetz)

Isolate the basic technical problem first, before working on it. Reducing difficulties to their simplest form makes practising them both more meaningful and more rewarding. A distinguished pianist once said that all technical difficulties are 'single-finger' problems.

Study not only the difficult passage, but the difficulty itself reduced to its most elementary principles. (Alfred Cortot)

Avoid at all costs the error of equating speed of execution with progress; music is not a race, to be won by the player who gets to the end of the piece first! Working only for greater speed simply reduces the gaps between the notes; it will do nothing to improve the quality of the notes themselves. A composer's most profound thoughts are more often to be found in his slower, contemplative works.

I believe that music must first and foremost stir the heart; this cannot be achieved by mere rattling and drumming. (C. P. E. Bach)

Practise or *perform*; don't get caught in the 'no man's land' in between, stopping, repeating the mistake once only, and then going on. Progress is made on a broad front if all aspects of technique are covered at every stage. Begin with very simple exercises in single-note playing, slurs, arpeggios, chords, etc., then after several days (or weeks), choose slightly more difficult versions of the same exercises and, continue the routine as before.

Technique is a vast empire; so wide are its fields that, unless ploughed, sown and reaped strategically, the yield will be poor, haphazard and disappointing. (Philippe Monnet)

Try, at an early stage of learning a piece, to imagine the finished performance. It is far harder and more time-consuming to attempt to apply 'expression' to a mechanically perfected piece which is devoid of musical feeling; technical habits must first be unlearned before a true interpretation can develop. Expression is not a mere finishing touch—it is an integral part of the music. In any case, preparing a genuinely expressive performance does not require much more work than a mindlessly technical one, if undertaken from the beginning.

Study the score away from the instrument, otherwise your fingers will make interpretative decisions for you. You should first be certain of your artistic purpose, then work out how to do it. (Barry Douglas)

But beware also of wasting time over finger exercises away from the guitar; these are useless for developing dexterity. You learn only what you practise, and finger gymnastics which have no direct relevance to actual playing improve nothing but your ability to perform finger gymnastics!

Whatever interpretative effect you may be striving for— forte, piano, crescendo, ponticello, tasto, etc.—slight exaggeration is always a good thing, just as an actor must declaim a little in order to project to the audience. What you imagine you are doing does not always reach the audience, since the hoped-for effect has already been half-heard mentally by the player. Performances which are closely modelled on those of another player tend to be just 'smudged carbon copies' of the original, with little feeling of musical purpose or sense of direction. Many guitarists habitually listen to recordings of well-known players, then base their own playing on what they hear. The most prominent features of any performance are often those which are in some way misconceived or ill-judged; they 'jar' the ear, thereby attracting the listener's attention. He then tends to absorb these mannerisms (for they are little more than that), and to imitate them.

A more sensible course when learning a new piece is to resist the temptation to listen to *any* performance of it 'just to see how it goes', until after you have read it through a good many times—perhaps even memorized it. You will thus avoid compounding your own faults with those of another player. If you experience some difficulty in getting the gist of a piece from one or two readings, then sight-reading and aural perception are obviously in need of attention.

Do not copy *slavishly* any performer, however distinguished. Be honest and sincere in your musical thoughts and interpretation; play a work as you feel it yourself, but in a style which fits the period and mood of the piece. (Evelyn Rothwell, oboist)

The amount of progress made for a given amount of practising-time depends on the quality and intensity of the work; more can be achieved in a shorter time by the methodical concentration on essentials and vital detail than by any amount of random or spasmodic work.

The purpose of practising an instrument is the pleasurable communication of music; not to dazzle or impress, nor to pile up neurotic pyrotechnics which lead more often to psychological compensation than to musicianship. Downpours of vacuous technique are so much unsung hail, soon melted; but if the heart is reached and touched, even in the simplest way, the experience will be cherished and remembered. (Philippe Monnet)

'Self-taught' players, having chosen to ignore the world's great storehouse of musical lore and wisdom, accumulated over many centuries and with contributions from countless musicians, from the humblest to those of towering genius, should perhaps note the humility in the following:

Bach is the father, we are the children. Those of us who do anything right learned it from him. Whoever does not own to this is a scoundrel. (Wolfgang Amadeus Mozart)

Let J. S. Bach himself, from whom even the greatest composers learned their art, have the last word. When asked in later life to divulge the secret of his mastery, he replied:

I worked hard! If you are as industrious as I was, you will be no less successful.

9

CONCLUSION

WHEN everything that can be said about technique has been said (and this book makes no claim to being exhaustive), the ultimate aim must be to forget about technique altogether, and just to *play*. While performing, making music should occupy all the thoughts and emotions; the technical detail which has been worked at through many hours of preparation must now be excluded. In any case, by then it is far too late to effect any changes or improvements!

The 'technically flawless' performance, like the genuine 'authentic' one, will, for the vast majority of guitarists, remain forever an unattainable ideal, but real commitment to the music and a wish to communicate its message are within the reach of all players, and will give far more pleasure to player and audience alike than any amount of virtuosic 'fireworks'.

Technical progress seems to get slower with the passing years. Like the diminishing fret-distances on a guitar finger-board, the higher you go, the smaller the steps. Ever-finer detail becomes increasingly important as the ear grows in sensitivity, this aural development holding the key to continuing technical progress. The nineteenth-century composer and pianist Busoni expressed the opinion that 'We could learn a great deal more than we do by listening intently to our own playing, by judging with the utmost severity every sound we produce, from the beginning to the end of the piece. How many artists, as well as pupils there are, who lose valuable time by working mechanically, that is to say, without thinking! They pay no more attention to the sounds they produce than does a deaf man!'

The playwright Ibsen advised dramatists that their job was not to answer questions, but merely to ask them—advice which could apply equally to teachers. If this book has raised as many fresh questions in the mind of the guitarist as it has attempted to answer, part at least of my purpose will have been achieved, for there can be no final set of answers to the many complex problems which the really intelligent student will encounter on the long road to mastery. Nor would he find genuine and lasting satisfaction if it ever became possible for him to sit back and say: 'Now at last I can play the guitar!'

Appendix I

WRITING FOR THE GUITAR:
Comments of a non-guitarist composer
Stephen Dodgson

Amongst composers who do not play it, the guitar seems to have the reputation of being difficult to write for. And Segovia's comment that very extensive revision has been required in all the music written for him by non-guitarists has had the opposite effect to the one intended. He meant, I am sure, to allay fears and to give encouragement to an unfettered fancy. Why, after all, be too concerned with technical considerations with such a sympathetic and masterly editor at hand?

And yet, if all those Latin composers with the idiom of a familiar instrument ringing in their ears still had to have their music reorganized by Segovia, what hope for the rest of us? The prospect is a little like that of never daring to let go of the nursemaid's hand. Somehow or other the non-playing composer must seek a healthy independence as soon as he can feel the courage for it. For even the most sympathetic guidance from the 'editing' guitarist will tend, albeit unconsciously, to channel the music into patterns familiar through existing repertoire. Furthermore, dependence on his editor must sooner or later prove an obstacle to any really personal discovery of the guitar's special sound-world.

The truth is that any composer who has developed a reasonably high level of general instrumental confidence can perfectly well train his thoughts to encompass the fundamental character of guitar technique. With tenacity, he should gradually find himself able to select concepts suited to the instrument and instinctively lay them out effectively. Such adjustments as are then proved necessary will not only be much smaller, but they will be much more realistically understood by the composer.

In fact, it is seldom in the smaller matters that any trouble arises. The resulting difference in sound after most such adjustments is minimal, and it is only reasonable that the non-playing composer should continue throughout his career, to require some experienced editorial assistance here. The dangers of a too heavy editorial reliance are more profound and, sadly, far commoner. All too often the result is the melancholy spectacle of a conscientious player searching desperately for a way to give idiomatic utterance to musical material which was instrumentally unsuitable in the first place.

In all probability, tonal, textural, and rhythmic notions, utterly distinct from those imagined for other instruments, will proliferate in the imagination in direct ratio to the development of this understanding. And this can only happen if the composer is willing to seek, and the players actively to encourage, an inside involvement in how the two hands cause the strings to sound. It is just possible that the aspiring composer might profit by some elementary instruction on the guitar, but I doubt it. He is likely to achieve more by careful observation, and by picturing the position of the hands vividly in his imagination. It is a question of learning to play the instrument *in the mind*. The composer who has absorbed the information collected in the earlier chapters of this book will already have received some valuable 'lessons' of this kind.

As regards the left hand, I have found a home-made chart of the fingerboard a useful piece of equipment. It needs to show the notes at each fret, and it should reproduce the proportional narrowing of the distance between frets in ascending. By pondering the positioning of the fingers, the stretches involved, the shifts between one chord and another, one gradually acquires a 'nose' for which chords will prove readily playable and in what spacing. During actual composition, this acquired instinct will soon prove a reliable guide to the fundamental practicability of the work as it progresses; no need to pause and check constantly on that account. Conversely, an instinctive caution will also develop, demanding a quick reference to the chart to investigate some more daring proposition that suddenly presents itself in the heat of composition.

It may take a little experience (and a piece or two) before such checks cease to seem an obstacle to invention. But it will

(*pace* Segovia) be an obstacle worth overcoming, since ultimately these lessons in the mind will stimulate hitherto unsus-
pected sonorities and figurations peculiar to the guitar, and of
good effect and strength of character. Examples 35 and 36

Ex. 35. Dodgson and Quine *Study No. 16*

Ex. 36. Dodgson and Quine *Study No. 6*

illustrate my own experience in this respect. The first of these
represents a type of organization familiar to guitarists, with a
melodic interest confined to a single string, ③, stopped at the
higher frets, possessing an intense quality because of the short
sounding-length, and heard above and among adjacent open
strings—an interesting sonority. The very notation betrays its
concept for the guitar and no other instrument. Example 36
may look initially less complex, yet it will be much less familiar
to most players. This is because it involves an unusual disposi-
tion of the right-hand fingers: the first finger is playing on ⑤ in
unaccustomed proximity to the thumb on ⑥. The musical
appeal lies in the emptiness of the bare intervals in their
somewhat gaunt spacing, and the avoidance of the three centre
strings.

The greatest temptation facing the novice is undoubtedly
that of writing too many notes, usually in a desire to achieve a
full sonority. Indeed, this temptation is so great that it seems
equally to assail the guitarist who also composes. In his case, if
the notes are lying there under his hand, why not employ

them? In the case of the non-player, the trouble is more likely
to be poor recognition of guitar resonance, how it develops and
what particular properties it has which may be profitably
stored in the memory. The notes in Example 37 look thin, as

Ex. 37 *Dodgson, London Lyrics No. 3* 'From a ship, tossing'

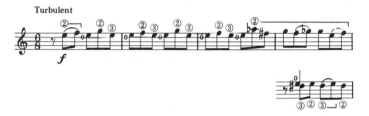

notes, but the fact that three strings are involved, that their
resonances overlap and interrupt each other, gives the sonority
an extraordinary richness and excitement, and is very characteristic of the guitar (see p. 73). Ask any player to demonstrate
the above extract as indicated, and then all on one string, and
the point will be vividly made. Such an experiment is also
likely to show how much rarer is the reverse requirement, i.e.
the drier sonority of single-string execution, in which every
resonance is necessarily stopped short by its successor.

Left to himself in the fingering of a piece, a player will tend
to categorize the text he sees. Is it a broken-chord type of
texture suggesting a resonant layout involving as many strings
as possible? Or is it the conjunct, scalic type of writing which
would profit by the more defined articulation of a maximum
amount of single-string execution? Wherever there is a genuine
choice and artistic ambiguity in the player's mind, the composer will certainly be asked for his opinion. Preferably, he
should have considered the question for himself in the first
place; and it is almost certainly true that he will have considered the point once his idiomatic consciousness has been
sufficiently awakened.

As the above paragraph implies, there are a great many
resonances constantly being heard in guitar performances
whose sounding-lengths exceed their written values. Some
editors have occasionally attempted to indicate these

sounding-lengths fully, but on the whole this is a mistake, resulting only in an over-complicated text. The editor, like the composer, cannot address himself to a musical dunderhead. These constant incidental resonances should be recognized and valued therefore, but they should not for the most part be included in the notation. For the composer, an occasional string-sign will serve to show the intention clearly enough; or, if he prefers, a verbal instruction could be given (eg 'maximum resonance', 'very clear—no overheld notes').

On the other hand, there is a great deal of slovenly notation to be found. Notes are often accorded a length which is impossible to sustain, and the composer has no more precise idea in writing them than to mean, with a vague optimism, 'hold it for as long as you can'. Slovenly notation usually indicates slovenly thinking, and will certainly be reflected in slovenly performance, since so many guitarists (in my experience) are slack about note lengths.

Ex. 38 Dodgson and Quine *Study No. 12*

Notation of the kind seen in Example 38 should only be written when longer notes (minims) can indeed be sustained whilst the moving part (quavers) is executed. Composers should recognize that a fully sustained three-part texture like this is rare in guitar writing. When it is written, a composer should at least be certain that he *hopes* all the notes can be sustained. It is really very discouraging for the conscientious player to discover that the question of sound had not been considered, let alone its practicability.

Equally, there is a great need, amongst players as much as composers, for greater precision with regard to short note-lengths and equivalent rests. Given the characteristic tendency to allow resonance to continue on any one string as long as it may, many a player is slow to appreciate that the right hand must not only sound the notes, but sometimes—as swiftly, and

Ex. 39. Dodgson *Fantasy–Divisions*

with equal rhythmic accuracy—damp them. This is particularly true where the texture is light and mercurial, and mainly single line (see Example 39). The semi-quaver rests must be made as apparent as the notes. Had I meant what I often seem to hear in this passage, I would have to have written

which is a totally different concept. Likewise, the notation in Example 40 also contains a very definite instruction about right-hand damping; for example, the minim *must* mean a rhythmic damping at the next barline. If guitar-players are inclined to be slack about these matters, composers must bear a more fundamental blame wherever their own imprecision has fostered it.

Ex. 40. Dodgson and Quine *Study No. 4*

The most obvious factor of guitar resonance concerns the sound of the open strings. Most idiomatic writing contains a good many, and there are composers who have resisted invitations to write for the guitar on the ground of the all too familiar tonal gravity set in motion by those powerful open Es, As and

Ds. (The objection diminishes as you rise.) The objection is reasonable as a reaction to the rather mindless indulgence in open-string writing in much vapid composition, but argues a real poverty of invention if it is to be seriously upheld. The sound of the open string is a vital and beautiful factor which it would be utterly perverse to avoid. But, equally, there is no built-in necessity for any open string *having* to be heard as a tonal gravity point. Rather, it is a case of valuing their special quality and usefulness; of realizing, for instance, how one briefly sounded open string can serve the double purpose of providing a point of richer resonance at the same time as allowing the left hand to take up a new position cleanly.

When, however, the bottom string is tuned down to D—the only frequent retuning employed on the guitar—there can really only be one aim, which is to employ this open-string length a good deal. The tonal power of D–A–d on the bottom three strings is the biggest and grandest resource of the instrument, and it makes little sense to employ the retuning unless to exploit this majestic possibility, and then probably in a movement of some substance. The effect is cumulative, as is proved in the frequently heard transcriptions of Bach's great violin chaconne, where this tuning assumes an almost hypnotic beauty. The retuning of the bottom string down to E flat—or even down to low C sharp or up to F—are possibilities to keep somewhere at the back of one's mind. In all cases, there has to be a self-evident idea involved in such a retuning, with the open string made a feature of the composition. Retunings higher up the instrument will certainly meet with resistance, the objection being that they throw the fingers into confusion for no benefit. It follows, therefore, that the more esoteric the proposed scordatura, the more single-minded must be the musical cause it is to serve.

Most of the discussion so far has, in its technical aspect, concerned the player's left hand. Unfortunately, it is much harder for the onlooker to observe the technique of the right hand. The individual movements are tiny, and largely hidden by the player's hand. The right hand divides itself into two elements: the bottom, which is the thumb (*p*), and the top, the first three fingers (*i, m, a*). The little finger is never used. If a four-note chord is sounded, the four playing fingers take a note each. If a five-note chord is sounded, it means (unless it is spread in such a way as not to seem a chord at all) that ⑥ will have to be omitted, for the thumb will need to strike two strings in quick succession: ⑤ and ④. The thumb may, and in a six-note chord quite often does, traverse all six strings in a spread so fast that you scarcely notice it (Chapter 4, p. 34 amplifies these points).

From this it will be seen that while the thumb will sometimes be found on the upper strings, it is rare to find *i*, *m*, and *a* situated lower than ④. Rapid repetitions on a single note are very characteristic and brilliant, but they are most frequently employed—partly for the foregoing reason—on the upper four strings. The tremolo is a particular repetition-pattern in which the thumb (on a lower string) plays the first of a rapid four-note group, while *i*, *m*, and *a* in succession reiterate a single note on a higher string. Even if a composer does not wish to use this device (so well known from Tarrega's *Recuerdos de la Alhambra*), it forms a valuable reference point concerning fundamental right-hand technique, and is a reminder of the quality and relative ease of rapid repetitions of one note. It also has to be remembered that it involves all four fingers, and therefore no other note can be added without wrecking the pattern.

Composers are often unwittingly led into writing two or more parts in divergent rhythmic groupings. Such things are of course frequent in all sorts of styles. To almost anyone except a guitarist, Example 41 looks very mild. Even the

Ex. 41

guitarist has no problem with his left hand, but the clear separation of the two rhythms is another matter altogether. In reality, this is a counterpoint between two hands, and, as such, a commonplace in keyboard music, but the guitarist will have to articulate it with the four fingers of one hand only. Bearing this in mind, it is a simple test for the non-player to try tapping it out on his table-top.

Trills, turns, and all other single-string ornaments on adjacent notes are not executed by the right hand at all, though many composers seem to imagine that they are. All such decorations are articulated by the rapid succession of left-hand fingers, with only the initial sound being struck by the right hand. They are consequently related to slurs (see p. 65), a very gentle and subtle effect. Any composer who indicates a *ff* trill gives himself away immediately! Once a composer has discovered the special qualities of the slur and related ornaments, he is likely to find his invention stimulated by them. There is a fascinating distinction between the stresses given to significant (initial) notes, and those which are not struck by the right hand at all. The fact that the right hand is not asked to strike every note in Example 42 is admittedly helpful at the given speed, but the manner in which the slurs are grouped is an integral part of the idea *in sound*.

Ex. 42. Dodgson *Duo for Cello and Guitar*

Part of the appeal of all slurs and ornaments on the guitar lies in their quietness. In an instrument of limited dynamic range, this has enormous colouristic value. It is worth remembering that it is in single-line music that the player has the widest dynamic and colouristic control over his music. It may take a little courage to write a single line only, but additional notes may prove to be counter-productive, since no melody really sings in all its expressive and dynamic shading if subordinate features are allowed to cramp either of the hands. Richness lies in the colour, not in the number of notes heard simultaneously, and the colour is greatest when the general level is quiet. It is definitely a mistake to think of the guitar (as many do, apparently) as first and foremost a harmonic instrument; a mistake, because it leads the innocent into writing too many notes.

The more obvious possibilities in guitar colouring, while less important than the paramount questions discussed so far, should spring as readily as possible to the composer's imagination. The so-called pizzicato, executed by the right-hand thumb while the flesh of the hand damps the string (a resemblance here to the 'harp' stop on the harpsichord), is a strongly contrasted tone colour which can be strikingly applied. It is associated above all with the lower strings; and players may assume that the composer does not intend it to continue into notes ascending above the stave. It is therefore important to indicate the extent of any pizzicato; and, since the right hand has to be displaced somewhat to execute it, remember that it can be awkward to make the transition very rapidly. It is part and parcel of every player's technique to vary the point of attack to reflect expressive purpose, and the contrast of sul tasto with sul ponticello (near the fingerboard and near the bridge, respectively) is a habitual device with which to highlight a repetition or echo effect. It is the equivalent of a change in scoring. When he wishes to make a contrast especially emphatic, the player will employ the *flesh* of the finger sul tasto, and, very decisively, the *nail* sul ponticello. Obviously, these colorations will be employed by players whether indicated or not, but if the composer has a strong contrast in mind, it will be good to show it.

The resonance of the instrument's body allows for a large number and variety of percussive effects, according to where it is struck, and whether the nail, the flesh of the finger, or the palm is used. Any player can quickly demonstrate most of the possibilities, starting with tambura—the only one in normal classical usage. Even tambura, though more 'musical' than the others, quickly loses its atmospheric appeal if overdone. Economy with all percussive effects certainly seems to be the best advice.

No stringed instrument is richer in the excellence of its harmonics. Both natural and artificial harmonics are readily obtainable and in great variety. Depending on the position in which the right hand finds itself, it is often possible to sound other notes (not in harmonics) at the same time. Provided that you can imagine vividly the effect of a passage involving harmonics—and there seems a chance of its proving possible—it is well worth writing it down and seeking a player's advice. The subtlety of hand positions is such that it is doubtful that the non-player could ever be completely sure which harmonic to choose when alternatives are available; and this leads me to believe that, unless you know for certain, it is best to show the note to be heard with *harm.* and the customary circle. Allow the player to investigate, and to write down his particular solution. Perhaps the most important point to stress is the surprising strength of (especially) the natural harmonics up to the double octave, and their uncanny beauty and length of resonance. They can have the effect of ringing on much longer than ordinary notes.

Most of the latter part of this discussion has concerned the subtle variations in technique which can enrich the expressive range of the guitar. As soon as the guitar is used in combination with other instruments, which almost invariably means with much more assertive instruments, many of these subtleties, so worth storing in the mind for solo use, are lost. Yet the guitar is a splendid instrument in the duo, trio, or quartet type of ensemble, and its potential here is still underexplored. Traditionally, its role has been humbly accepted as a natural accompanist, gracefully allowing the melody instruments to dominate. As soon as the guitar is given a more independent and characterful part—even for a few bars—it is essential to consider the question of balance more deeply and at an early stage in the compositional process. The two most practical observations I can offer are (1) that a rhythmic characteristic, distinct in itself, is a great help; and (2) so is an equally decisive contrast of register. That is to say, the guitar should be heard as an important voice, providing the other simultaneous sounds are quite different rhythmically and are kept well clear of the vital compass. Apart from this, it is perhaps almost superfluous to add that the composer's skill in writing transparently for the partnering instruments is in truth the nub of the matter; but even with the greatest skill, the full colouristic range of the guitar will only become evident when given, momentarily, the field to itself. Amplification, to my mind, can sometimes assist a goodish balance to be better, but it will never produce a gratifying result when relied upon to do the whole job.

Fundamentally, my wish in this chapter is simply to encourage composers to write for the guitar. Huge as the repertoire already is, good music for the instrument will undoubtedly be welcomed, and its composer flooded with invitations to write more. But I do not believe that this can happen without his trying to 'get inside' the instrument for himself. Moreover, I believe that the effort of doing so will be rewarded by an abundance of new ideas, increasingly idiomatic as experience accumulates. Lastly, and perhaps most importantly of all, the non-playing composer does have the advantage of being, in essence, free of all the more commonplace patterns of the instrument; and this is exactly why the serious guitarist needs, and will welcome, his involvement.

Appendix II

REPERTOIRE

The quantity of published music for solo guitar is so vast that
any attempt at compiling a comprehensive list would be to
undertake a near-impossible task; it would also need another
volume at least equal in size to this present one. Unfortunately, quantity is not matched by quality, and even to sift
the few grains of wheat from so much chaff seemed so daunting
that I decided not to attempt it, but to publish instead a
personal selection of music which I consider to be of sufficient
substance and musical interest for inclusion in a serious solo
guitar recital, and which would give pleasure to an informed
and cultured audience. I do not mean to imply that music
which is not included is therefore of inferior quality; such a
relatively short list as this can only contain a representative
selection—specimens as guide-lines to programme-building.

The performance of transcriptions borrowed from the reper-
toires of other instruments is a controversial matter on which
opinions differ widely at the present time. For this reason I
have decided not to give a detailed list of pieces, and the notes
which follow are intended only as a general indication of
categories of transcription which may be more acceptable.

The lute works of Bach form an indispensable corner-stone
of the guitar's 'borrowed' repertoire; no recital in which ba-
roque music is included would be complete without it. This
music, written for the guitar's 'cousin', adapts readily in both
technique and spirit, as also do most of Bach's compositions
for unaccompanied violin or cello. Renaissance lute music, too,
transcribes well and loses little of its nobility when played on
the guitar. The more substantial works of Dowland, Cutting,
Johnson, da Milano, etc. find a legitimate place in a recital.
programme;Dowland's Fantasies or his *Lachrimae Antiquae
Pavan*, for example, deserve to rank with the finest music for
any instrument of the period.

The music written for the guitar's other 'cousin'—the

vihuela—though mainly simpler in construction than the lute works, has dignity and charm, and fits naturally into the early part of a chronologically arranged guitar recital programme. While a number of pieces from these sources are excellent music, many are short and lacking in substance, so careful selection is necessary when deciding what to transcribe.

Transcriptions of keyboard music are more problematical, and my own view is that only those dozen or so sonatas by Scarlatti which adapt well to the guitar sound entirely convincing. Few other pieces which were written originally for the keyboard are totally satisfying as guitar arrangements. My general advice to guitarists who wish to perform a transcription in a public recital is that they should first ask themselves whether the music sounds better—or at least as good—on the guitar as it did on the original instrument. If there is any doubt over this question, then don't play it!

The nineteenth century provides a numerically rich source of original guitar works, though the quality of most of it is on a much lower musical plane, consisting mainly of 'salon pieces' composed largely by amateurs. A brief comparison with the work of the major composers of the period immediately exposes its threadbare nature. It is probably best omitted altogether from public performances, though certain technical studies are valuable for private practising. Much of the original guitar music composed in the early years of this century, too, is really only pastiche, written in nineteenth-century style to accord with the tastes of one particular player. Again, very careful selection is needed, but a few examples of this genre will be found in the following list.

The above critical 'weeding-out' process has substantially reduced the vast quantity of published guitar music, so that all that remains is original compositions of the last fifty years, and this forms the bulk of my personal selection. Taken together with the recommendations mentioned above, this provides the solo guitar with more than enough music of substance and quality.

The rumoured 'coming decline' of the guitar does not need to happen, for developments during the next twenty or thirty years could see dramatic improvement in its musical status if guitarists will address themselves to the real challenges and opportunities. That the instrument's repertoire holds the key to the future, there can be little doubt. Professor Smith Brindle sums this up succinctly:

The reason behind the decline seems certain to be due to a falling-off of audience interest, caused principally by the lack of real musical substance in programmes. Players tend to gravitate towards shallow and banal music which shows off their techniques without saying anything profound. Guitarists must stop playing infantile trifles, and respond to the challenge.

The guitar's improved musical status will, I believe, depend increasingly on its integration into other forms of music, particularly as a member of chamber ensembles, or as a concerto soloist. I have therefore listed some of the, as yet not too plentiful, original works which include it. The list is not exhaustive as arrangements and adaptations have been excluded; neither is all the music necessarily of the finest quality, but it is a beginning! Guitarists who are not uncompromisingly immersed in the overfished waters of solo playing, and who have an eye on the future, would be well-advised to try and gain some experience in this field.

Works for Solo guitar

Apostel, H., *Sechs Musiken*, Op. 25 (Universal).
Arnold, M., *Fantasy for Guitar*, Op. 107 (Faber).
Bach, J. S., *Lute Suite No. 1 in E minor* (Hofmeister).
—— *Lute Suite No. 2 in C minor* (A minor) (Hofmeister).
—— *Lute Suite No. 3 in G minor* (A minor) (Hofmeister).
—— *Lute Suite No. 4 in E major* (Hofmeister).
—— *Prelude, Fugue, and Allegro in E flat* (D) (Hofmeister).
—— *Chaconne* (Violin Partita No. 2 in D minor (Schott).
—— *Prelude and Fugue* (Violin Sonata No. 1 in G minor) (A minor) (Oxford University Press).
Bennett, R. R., *Five Impromptus* (Universal).
Berkeley, L., *Theme and Variations* (Bèrben).
Britten, B., *Nocturnal*, Op. 70 (Faber).
Carter, E., *Changes* (Boosey and Hawkes).
Castelnuovo-Tedesco, M., *Sonata* (*Omaggio a Boccherini*) (Schott).

Davies, P. M., *Lullaby for Ilian Rainbow* (Boosey and Hawkes).
—— *Hill Runes* (Boosey and Hawkes).
Dodgson, S., *Partita No. 1* (Oxford University Press).
—— *Partita No. 2* (Oxford University Press).
—— *Fantasy-Divisions* (Bèrben).
Falla, M. de., *Hommage à Debussy* (Chester).
Fricker, P. R., *Paseo* (Faber).
Gerhard, R., *Fantasia* (Mills).
Halffter, C., *Codex No. 1* (Universal).
Henze, H. W., *Drei Tentos* (Schott).
—— *Royal Winter Music I* (Sonata) (Schott).
—— *Royal Winter Music II* (Sonata) (Schott).
Hoddinott, A., *Sonatina*, Op. 98 No. 1 (Oxford University Press).
Krenek, E., *Suite* (Doblinger).
Martin, F., *Quartre Pièces Brèves* (Universal).
McCabe, J., *Canto* (Novello).
Mompou, F., *Suite Compostelana* (Éditions Salabert).
Petrassi, G., *Nunc* (Suvini Zerboni).
Rawsthorne, A., *Elegy* (Oxford University Press).
Rodrigo, J., *Invocation and Dance* (Universal).
Smith Brindle, R., *El Polifemo de Oro* (Bruzzichelli).
Stoker, R., *Sonatina*, Op. 42 (Bèrben).
Swayne, G., *Suite* (Novello).
Takemitsu, T., *Folios* (Éditions Salabert).
Tippett, M., *The Blue Guitar* (Schott).
Turina, J., *Sonata* (Schott).
Villa-Lobos, H., *Douze Études* (Eschig).
Walton, W., *Five Bagatelles* (Oxford University Press).
Wills, A., *Sonata* (Oxford University Press).
—— *Suite Africana* (Oxford University Press).
—— *Moods and Diversions* (Bèrben).

Chamber works with guitar

Apostel, H., *Trio* ('Little Chamber Concerto') (fl., va., gtr.).
Arnold, M., *Serenade* (gtr. and str.) (Patterson).
Badings, H., *Trio No. 9* (fl., va., gtr.) (Donemus).
Beethoven, L. van, *Serenade* (vn., va., gtr.).

Boccherini, L., *Quintet No. 1 in D minor* (gtr. and str. qt.) (Suvini Zerboni).

—— *Quintet No. 2 in E major* (gtr. and str. qt.) (Suvini Zerboni).

—— *Quintet No. 3 in B flat major* (gtr. and str. qt.) (Suvini Zerboni).

—— *Quintet No. 4 in D major* (gtr. and str. qt.) (Suvini Zerboni).

—— *Quintet No. 5 in D major* (gtr. and str. qt.) (Suvini Zerboni).

—— *Quintet No. 6 in G major* (gtr. and str. qt.) (Suvini Zerboni).

Bozza, E., *Concertino da Camera* (gtr. and str. qt.) (United Music Publishers).

Call, L. de, *Trio* (fl., va., gtr.).

Castelnuovo-Tedesco, M., *Quintet* (gtr. and str. qt.) (Schott).

—— *Eclogues* (fl., c.a., gtr.) (Schirmer).

Dodgson, S., *Sonata for Three* (fl., va., gtr.) (Éditions Orphée).

Gerhard, R., 'Libra' (fl., cl., vn., perc., pf. gtr.).

Giuliani, M., *Quintet*, Op. 65 (vn.1, vn.2, va., vc., gtr.) (Simrock).

Haydn, J., *Quartet* (vn., va., vc., gtr.).

Kreutzer, J., *Trio* (fl., cl., gtr.).

Henze, H. W., *Kammermusik 1958 for Tenor, Guitar and Eight Solo Instruments* (Schott).

Matiegka, W., *Serenade*, Op. 26 (fl., va., gtr.).

—— *Quartet* (fl., va., vc., gtr.).

Molino, F., *Trio in D*, Op. 45 (fl., va., gtr.) (Schott).

Musgrave, T., *Sonata for Three* (fl., vn., gtr.) (Novello).

Paganini, N., *Quartet No. 7* (vn., va., vc., gtr.) (Peters).

—— *Terzetto Concertante* (vn., vc., gtr.) (Zimmerman).

Patten, J., 'In Memory of Anne' (fl., va., gtr.).

Spinner, L., *Quintet*, Op. 14 (cl., hn., bn., d.-b., gtr.) (Boosey and Hawkes).

Weber, C. M. von, *Minuet in A* ('Donna Diana') (fl. va., gtr.).

Webern, A., *Two Pieces*, Op. 19 (S.A.T.B., Celeste., vn., cl., bass cl., gtr.).

Concertos for guitar and orchestra

Arnold, M., *Concerto for Guitar and Strings*, Op. 67 (Faber).

Bennett, R. R., *Concerto for Guitar and Chamber Ensemble* (Universal).

Berkeley, L., *Guitar Concerto*, Op. 88 (Chester).

Castelnuovo Tedesco, M., *Concerto in D*, Op. 99 (Schott).

—— *Concerto Sereno in C*, Op. 160 (Schott).

Carulli, F., *Concerto in A major* (Bèrben).

Giuliani, M., *Concerto in A for Guitar and Strings*, Op. 30 (Ricordi).

Dodgson, S., *Concerto No. 1 for Guitar and Chamber Orchestra* (Bèrben).

—— *Concerto No. 2 for Guitar and Chamber Orchestra* (Bèrben).

Haug, H., *Concertino for Guitar and Small Orchestra* (Bèrben).

Ponce, M., *Concierto del Sur* (Schott).

Rodrigo, J., *Concierto de Aranjuez* (Schott).

—— *Fantasia para un Gentilhombre* (Schott).

Villa-Lobos, H., *Concerto for Guitar and Small Orchestra* (Schott).